The Reluctant Vegetarian Cookbook

An Easy Introduction to Cooking Without Meat, Eggs, and Other Once-Favorite Foods and Discovering What Tastes Even Better

By Sharalyn Pliler
Illustrations by Genevra Daly

authorHOUSE®

AuthorHouse™
1663 Liberty Drive
Bloomington, IN 47403
www.authorhouse.com
Phone: 1-800-839-8640

First published by AuthorHouse 7/2/2009

ISBN: 978-1-4389-8520-6 (e)
ISBN: 978-1-4389-8519-0 (sc)

Printed in the United States of America
Bloomington, Indiana

This book is printed on acid-free paper.

Dedication

To the farmers, sellers, purchasers, organizers, activists,
and anyone who contributes in whatever way
to providing, preserving, and treasuring
fresh, natural, pure foods.

We are What We Eat

Fifty percent of the profits from this book will be donated to organizations that work to provide and protect pure foods.

TABLE OF CONTENTS

Acknowledgements

Many people helped set the table and prepare the meals that made this book possible, and to them I owe great thanks.

Thanks first of all to the many reluctant vegetarians who encouraged me to write this book by asking questions and asking for recipes. Special thanks goes to Mary Shinn who said, "Yours is the only food I can eat that doesn't give me indigestion." Admittedly, her happy tummy probably had more to do with the vegetarian and Ayurvedic style of preparation than it did to my cooking, but her comment gave me the courage to believe I should write this book.

Thanks to Ed Hipp, former director of the kitchens at Maharishi University of Management in Fairfield, Iowa, who created the original masterpiece, *Un-chicken Soup*, which inspired me with the understanding that tofu and other foods could make familiar meaty tastes.

Thanks to my grandmother, who cooked amazing meals on a big black wood-fired stove and who by example taught me old-fashioned cooking savvy.

Thanks also to my parents, to my father who encouraged a hunger for education, and to my mother, who despite frequent reservation in regard to my life's adventures, supported me in many ways, including loaning me money to attend college.

Thanks to Steve Hutchins for writing advice, Genevra Daley for the artwork, and Alan in Oz for kicking my butt to get this book finished.

Special thanks to Nic Martel at Authorhouse for the great layout and design work.

Thanks, unendingly, for the personal and professional growth that came from Maharishi Mahesh Yogi's Transcendental Meditation program and Maharishi University of Management's Master's in Professional Writing Program. I don't know that I meet up to their standards but I do know that without them, this book would never have been written; I would have remained a dreamer instead of becoming a writer.

Finally, thanks to you for being adventurous enough to give this book and a new diet style a try.

CHAPTER 1
How an Omnivore Became a Vegetarian

"But I don't want to be a vegetarian!"

"Who in their right mind would ever become a vegetarian?" I mused to myself as I turned sizzling pork chops in a cast-iron skillet and feasted on the meaty aroma. Pork chops were my favorite meal. When I say pork chops, I mean just pork chops, nothing else. Like many other people, I considered vegetables to be merely decoration for the meat. At family gatherings where the table groaned with the typical Ozark farm country meat, bread and potatoes, some relative would say, "Oh, yes, we need a vegetable, how about some canned peas?" Such afterthought vegetables were usually seasoned with bacon or ham to, "give them some flavor," as Grandma said. As children, we ate vegetables dutifully. "They're good for you," Mom insisted. "Yuck," I remember thinking, "how could anything that tastes so dull be good for you?"

If, at the moment I was turning those pork chops, someone had told me that before the next Thanksgiving I would become a vegetarian, I would have had a hearty laugh to go with my meal—possibly garnished with a few choice words for the person who suggested it. Give up all the great tasting meat foods for wimpy veggies? Don't be ridiculous.

Over the next few years the memory of that moment and my supercilious disdain was to come back to me on more than one occasion as I ate a new dish called "crow" or—if you prefer it in vegetarian language—"humble pie."

How I—Reluctantly—Became a Vegetarian

I became a vegetarian by the only route open to someone with a closed mind, by accident. It happened in the early '70's when I was on a hippie trip in my customized Volkswagen van. I'd built a bed on one side, bookshelves on the other, packed a tambourine, a typewriter, and a plastic port-a-potty along with such foods that would keep without refrigeration and be easy to cook on a propane stove, then set out for parts unknown.

"Hippie fling," my stern-eyed aunt called my trip. I steamed a little under her withering gaze but kept on going. I wasn't sure at the time what the trip should be called, I just knew I needed to find my own direction, to find out who I was out without alarm clocks, social mandates, friends, or family. Years later, reading about Native Americans' customs, I would understand that the trip might best be called a vision quest, and I would always be glad I did it. I believe everyone needs to have a vision quest.

But, by whatever name the journey might be called, I certainly didn't anticipate that becoming a vegetarian would be one of the outcomes.

I was in fact seriously worried about what would happen to me on a no-meat diet while I camped in the wilderness the first couple of weeks of the trip. Would I become weak? I pictured myself, alone, starved to skin and bones, crawling on hands and knees, finally collapsing on the trail. Months later, hikers would find my skeleton. I reminded myself sternly that if I started feeling weak I should cut the trip short, get back to civilization and get some decent food.

Unexpected Consequences

After leaving my Southwest Missouri "stomping grounds," as one's home area is called in Native American territory, I drove around for a few days in the four-state region looking for the right spot to park my VW. My goal was to find a place to camp where I could turn in a complete circle and see nothing man-made. Somewhere in the vicinity of Fox, Arkansas, I found myself driving down miles of gravel road cut through pastures and dense woods. Suddenly I saw a break in the trees. It was an old two-rut trail, its overgrown grass indicating that it was little if ever used now. I eased the van into it.

After a half-mile of winding, narrow, weed-grown lane, I spotted an isolated clearing, not perfect because there was a man-made pond in the view, but good enough. Careful not to disturb the ground, I worked the van around until it was level enough that I would at least not fall out of bed from the tilt, and set up housekeeping.

It's an interesting thing, being alone. Even though I'd had no fear of being alone in the city, I discovered that being completely alone in the woods was a different matter. At night, I experienced primal fears, even imagining swamp monsters, dripping in muddy horror, staggering out of the pond. I would tell myself, "Don't be silly!" But for the first few days, I was mighty glad to see daybreak, when just a touch of morning sun made nonsense of such fantasies. I'd remind myself that to be acknowledged as warriors, Native American youths had to survive alone in the woods for a week. I had none of their survival skills, but if a teenager could face being alone, surely I, with a van and it's safety and conveniences, could too.

Despite imaginary woo-woos lurking in the shadows, I began feeling a harmony with life. It began to sink in that nature and humans were not separate, as in us versus them, but in fact we were all part of the same marvelous creation. If there was such a thing as swamp monsters, perhaps I should invite them to one of my out-of-the-box macaroni and cheese suppers.

To my surprise, not only did I lose the fear of swap monsters, the fear of dying of starvation on a no-meat diet also proved to be merely from an overworked and under-educated imagination. Within three or four days I was amazed to experience that instead of getting weaker without meat, just the opposite happened—I felt more energetic, lighter and more clear-headed, and despite the increased physical activity of hikes in the woods, I needed to eat less quantity than before. Most amazing of all, I found (despite the overall poor-quality foods I had packed for the trip) that food tasted better, as if my taste buds had come alive.

Had this greater strength, clarity and pleasure I'd been experiencing come from not eating meat?

At the end of the week, watching the sunset change from a brilliant orange and magenta to rhinestone stars sparkling on blues and blacks, I struggled to understand what had happened to me. I'd questioned many things in life but it had never occurred to me before then to question beliefs about the foods we eat.

I asked myself, had this greater strength, clarity and pleasure I'd been experiencing come from not eating meat?

I didn't want to ask that question because in my heart I already knew the answer—it was yes. I tried to argue with myself that maybe a vacation in the fresh air away from the grind of modern life was sufficient to account for it, or maybe it was from the extra exercise.

But it wouldn't play. It was obvious that the change I'd experienced was deeper than what could have come from a mere vacation. I finally had to admit it, my body's reaction to a week on a meatless diet was enthusiastically positive.

Me, a Vegetarian? No Way!

My heart sank. I didn't *want* to be a vegetarian. I *liked* the taste of meat foods—tacos, pizzas, spaghetti, and, of course, pork chops. But worse than giving up favorite foods was the thought of being an oddball. I liked thinking of myself as a daring, groundbreaking hippie radical who broke down social conventions in order to bring the world into peace and harmony...but apparently my courage to be different only applied to strangers. I quailed at the thought of being seen by my peers as being too weird. Hadn't I only a few months earlier defined vegetarians as being *not in their right minds*?

At the time, medical and nutritional authorities advised eating plenty of meat for a healthy diet; textbooks advised eating it at least once a day; mother served it; fast food was centered around it—meat was everywhere. Even in hippie days, in my social group, anyone that wouldn't die for hamburgers, greasy tacos, or sausage pizza was considered strange.

Yet, no matter how much I might not *want* to be a vegetarian, how could I argue with the direct experience of feeling so good after a week of no meat?

Struggling with this dilemma, I made a campfire. The friendly crackling flames made good company as I sat poking a stick into them, searching my memory for anything I knew about vegetarianism—bits and pieces of information I'd picked up from a yoga book, articles in *National Geographic* about different cultures, and books on vegetarianism that had passed mostly ignored under my disdainful nose. I recalled that I'd briefly scanned, scorned and dismissed the whole idea, tossing it, with the pseudo-intellectual arrogance of youth, into such mental categories as *primitive oddities*, *religious fanaticism*, and *silly customs*.

I remembered curling my lip at the idea stated in a yoga book that only those who eat non-meat foods could become spiritually enlightened. At the time I interpreted this information as religious dogma slanted by cultural bias. Much later I would learn that worldwide, many different cultures and religions have advocated a meatless diet, including not only Buddhists and Hindus but ancient Christian Gnostics and modern Mormons. Having experienced how good I felt on a no-meat diet, I had to wonder, could it be that *I* was the one with the cultural bias?

Staring at the flickering campfire, I realized there might be genuine truth to the yogi's claim, for without the heaviness of meat in my system, I actually did feel en-*light*-ened—lighter in both mind and body. Plus, I'd experienced that I needed to eat less yet was feeling more energetic. Wouldn't this suggest that the body has to work harder to digest meat, thus diverting energy from the mental/spiritual aspects of growth and development to the lower function of mere physical digestion?

Even if viewed only as a physical health issue, logic argued, if the body had to work harder in order to digest meat, then didn't it make sense that it was *not* in the best interests of the body to eat it? Much later I'd learn that researchers believe the human body was not designed to eat meat. Comparing the differences between the teeth and digestive tracts of carnivorous animals and man, studies found that where animals had sharp teeth and short digestive tracks to tear their food and digest it quickly, the flatter teeth and longer digestive tracks of humans are superior designs for digesting grains and vegetables.

> ***I had to confront yet a larger truth, and that was that the beings we ate were not* things *like books, rocks or building materials, but members of our own family tree.***

Watching a spark from the campfire flicker into the star-strewn darkness, I recalled reading that in other parts of the world, whole societies were vegetarian. My assumption when I read about this had been that these must be primitive people who simply had not progressed into the 20th Century. But now sitting in front of my campfire with my body and mind feeling so good from a meatless diet, I wondered, with a sense of astonishment, if it was possible that the truth was actually the other way around—could it be that it was more primitive to eat meat? Had mankind as a whole simply not yet discovered the benefits of vegetarianism?

Beyond the night sounds of cicadas, frogs, and the whispers of wind though pine boughs, I heard a hound bay, and off in the distance, another answered. Was it like that for us humans, where we call out to each other as we struggle to find our way through the mysteries of our lives? Had we, generation after generation, reassured each other that it was not only okay but *necessary* to eat meat—when, in fact, meat actually wasn't good for us?

Forced now to consider this question, I had to confront yet a larger truth that needed to be considered, and that was that the beings we ate were not *things* like books, rocks or building materials, but were members of our own family tree. Memories came back to me how I felt as a young child, being told that I was eating the flesh of a once-living being. I'd been horrified. I knew from living on my grandparents' farm that these beings were like me because they had eyes, ears, teeth, skin, and hair—the same body parts, simply arranged differently. They looked at me with big soulful eyes and nuzzled me affectionately. Just like human beings, they nurtured their young, cried in pain and bled red blood when they were cut.

When I protested against eating them, my mother told me that God made animals for us to eat and if we didn't eat them, they'd overrun the earth like cows did in India.

Perhaps because I liked the taste of meat, I rationalized that if Mom and all these other adults thought it is okay, then it must be okay.

Now, in the woods as an adult, I wondered—could it be that in their innocence, children recognize that eating animals, our biological kin, is a form of cannibalism?

Willing to look at reality with fresh eyes, I recalled my experience with the live animals that later would be served on the table—calves sucking my fingers like human babies sucking a pacifier, and baby goats baaing and bouncing like jack-in-the-boxes while my brothers and I squealed with delight. We laughed uproariously watching pigs get glassy eyed with pleasure at being scratched on their bellies, and tried not to hear the piteous mooing of mother cows whose babies had been taken away from them, their grief and longing as unmistakable as the wailing of a human who had lost her child. We also tried to ignore it when grandpa chopped off the heads of chickens, their headless bodies filled with adrenaline's fight or flight flapping frantically around the farmyard long after their decapitation.

The truth, I had to admit, was that animals experience the same emotions that I did—pleasure and play, love and the need for love, fear, pain and fatigue ... the difference was only in degree. Seeing it, the thought suddenly came to me that we don't eat developmentally lesser humans, so what gives us the right to eat animals just because they are less developed?

Taking it one step further, I asked myself, if the life force in a human being is sacred, then how could the life force in an animal be any less sacred?

It was this last thought that brought me over the edge to a new life. Just as I would not eat my human brother, I could no longer eat my little brothers in evolution.

I tossed my stick into the fire. The decision was made. I had become a vegetarian.

CHAPTER 2
Learning a New Diet Style

Is there life after giving up meat?

To my surprise, in the thirty years that have passed since I reluctantly became a vegetarian, whenever I tell others I am a vegetarian the response has *not* been, "Are you out of your mind?' In fact, I have been inspired to write this book because so many people have said to me, "I'd really like to eat less meat, but I don't know what else to fix."

I know how they feel. Driving the van out of the woods back to "civilization," I felt so much better that I knew my decision to become a vegetarian had been the right thing to do. But I also realized I didn't know beans about a meatless diet. What do vegetarians do for a main dish? What if they want a sandwich? What do they eat at restaurants? How do they know if they're getting a balanced diet? What works for taste satisfaction?

Driving past McDonalds, Taco Bell and all my old meat haunts, my taste habits made me long for a good ole' taco, burger or pizza. But every time I thought about actually eating meat, my stomach protested. Put that greasy, heavy stuff in my body after the great experience I'd had in the woods without it? No way.

But what else was there to eat? Like many new vegetarians, my diet was terrible for the first few months. Until I became a vegetarian, my acquaintance with non-meat foods had been limited to white bread, cheese (as in processed cheese-sandwiches and powdered cheese in macaroni-and-cheese), boiled beans, salads, canned vegetables, and, of course, potatoes at every meal. How much more boring could one get? Reluctant to admit I didn't have a clue, for a while I lived primarily on granola, salads and milk.

New Learning

But hungry for something more to eat, I finally decided to see what others had to say on the subject. Thumbing through various books on vegetarianism at a bookstore as I passed through Atlanta, Georgia, I found myself overwhelmed and intimidated by lecturing tones, a lot of do's and don't's, and unfamiliar foods such as millet and tofu. In dietary culture shock, I left the bookstore without buying anything. Looking back now, I know it would have served me better to have been a lot more open-minded.

Discovering that Properly Cooked Vegetables Taste (Not Merely Good but) Great

Fortunately, a major breakthrough happened when I had lunch at a good vegetarian restaurant. In St. Petersburg, Florida, a couple of weeks later, I inquired of the locals if they could direct me to one. I entered the Bo Tree feeling as suspicious as a chicken at a slaughterhouse, as if maybe these people might try to brainwash me into believing in their brand of vegetarianism. But once inside, I found a homey ambiance I'd eventually learn is characteristic of many mom-and-pop vegetarian places. It really felt inviting but I still wasn't wholly reassured that it was safe. I sat at one of the tables covered with clean, red-and-white checkered tablecloth with a charming little vase containing a couple of daises.

Tentatively, I admitted to the waitress that I didn't know anything about vegetarianism so I didn't know what to order. She smiled and recommended a sautéed dish.

While I waited for my order, I glanced around to see what other vegetarians looked like. Oddly enough, they looked like me—longhaired hippies with bellbottoms and tie-dyed T-shirts. They didn't look weird or out of the ordinary; no one looked "out of his mind" or out of touch with reality, at least not any more than did the average hippie. The wait for the food was longer than at McDonald's or other factory-food places, but as I was to learn, good food is worth waiting for.

Unlike the processed, pre-prepared, additive-laced, store-bought, cooked-as-an-afterthought, prepared-as-a-mere-dressing-for-the-meat kind of vegetables I had eaten in the past, each vegetable in this glorious dish tasted unique and special.

When the waitress came back, she set before me a beautiful plate of vegetables.

I'm sure that she and the cook had no idea what pivotal roles they were to play in my life. The plate of veggies she served made such an impact that that it has set the standard for my own cooking to this day, eventually becoming one of the cornerstones for this book.

It was an artwork of broccoli, carrots, potatoes, green peppers, cabbage—all sautéed to lively perfection, rich in color, texture, and flavor, not smothered in meat sauce or cooked into dullness. Unlike the processed, pre-prepared, additive-laced, store-bought, cooked-as-an-afterthought, prepared-as-a-mere-dressing-for-the-meat kind of vegetables I had eaten in the past, each vegetable in this glorious dish tasted unique and special. Each proudly announced itself to my taste buds,

"I'm broccoli!" "I'm carrots!" "I'm cabbage!" My whole mouth seemed to come alive with these "new" flavors—hearty, filling, tasty and tantalizing. Unlike the limp vegetables I had been familiar with, these had rich, full, varied aromas, tastes, textures, and rich, appetizing colors.

As I ate, I began to feel a deep-down satisfaction in my tummy. Astonished, I thought to myself, *this is the taste satisfaction that all of us looked for in meat, but it isn't meat that gives it to us—it's the vegetables.* By making meat the mainstay and vegetables the afterthought, by dulling our senses and our taste buds with the residue of meat, our meat-centered culture had failed to recognize or fully experience how wonderful and satisfying vegetables really are.

Experiencing New Vistas

In the woods, experiencing the physical and mental benefits of a no-meat diet, I had sold out to not eating meat; now at the Bo Tree, with my tummy humming its thanks, I found myself sold out to vegetables themselves.

Before the Bo Tree, I had never been more than a utilitarian "meat and potatoes" cook. But my experience at the Bo Tree left me wanting to know how to create this taste delight for myself. The chef appreciated my praise and answered my eager questions.

Fresh

"Always begin with fresh vegetables," he said for openers, "the fresher the better. Put them into a sauté pan with good butter or olive oil."

I waited, expecting for him to say more.

"Stir them so they don't burn, and don't overcook them."

I was still waiting for the hard part.

He pushed back the checkered cloth that separated the dining room and his pungent-smelling kitchen, and then turned for one last piece of advice. "Oh, yeah." He said, wiping his hands on his apron, "experiment with herbs."

That's all there was to getting such great tasting food? I had eaten of the fruits of the earth, pure, fresh food, cooked with love, and to my amazement it had been the best meal I had ever eaten ... and it was all so simple?

More Taste Adventure

A couple of weeks later, headed for Key West, I was looking for a nice ocean side spot at Key Largo to eat some lunch (probably granola and milk) when I saw a young hippie couple who had set up camp. They'd connected sapling poles covered with a tie-dyed cloth to their VW van to create shade for a small camp stove and two canvas folding chairs.

Except for a warm smile and worn blue jeans (the hippie uniform of the day) the man was naked—no shoes, no shirt, just service. The woman, radiant with youth and the beauty of new motherhood, wore a peasant-style dress. Both had long brown hair. Three days earlier, she'd given birth and they where hanging out to give Mama and baby a chance to rest and recuperate. The baby, cradled in the mother's arms on a blue blanket, was pink with sunburn. "I didn't realize that he wasn't used to being in the sun," the mother explained with a rueful tone. She didn't look to be more than late teens or early twenties. We chatted briefly about how we came to be here, where we were going and the hippie scene in general.

"We were just getting ready to eat," the no-longer strangers said easily. "Want to join us?"

I responded (now with a little feeling of pride to have discovered something so important),"Oh, thanks, I'd love to, but I have just become a vegetarian."

"Oh, great," she said happily. "We're vegetarians too." I was instantly curious to know what they ate, but judging by their battered old van and shabby clothes, I doubted they could afford another mouth. "Thanks, I said, "but I'll move on."

"Just have a bite then," the petite young woman said, handing the baby to her husband. From a tray in the van, she handed me two Ritz-type crackers.

Like many people, I had fearfulness about trying new foods, but when I saw those crackers, what I felt was closer to panic. They were covered with something that might have been from the feast scene which, looking back later, have come from the movie, *Indiana Jones and the Temple of Doom.* Oozing off the edges of cracker was some kind of brackish-brown mash with green and red lumps.

Apparently my horrified reluctance showed on my face.

"It's lentils," the young mom said reassuringly, as if I might actually know what lentils were. "Go ahead, try it; it tastes like tacos."

Tacos? Oh, how much I been missing the taste of tacos. But my mood at the moment was that if I had to put something that strange looking into my mouth in order to get a taco taste, perhaps I should wait a lot longer.

However, rather than appear as cowardly as I actually was, and rather than hurt this sweet lady's feelings by rejecting her gift, I gathered up the courage to bite into that unnerving mass.

What happened next was shocking. It tasted *good*. It tasted *really* good. I was utterly amazed. It tasted so meaty, so flavorful—*but without the heaviness of meat.* Somehow it tasted more like tacos than meat tacos did. Shifting from reluctance to enthusiasm, I scrambled mentally to think how could I get myself re-invited to lunch.

What happened next was shocking. It tasted good. It tasted* really *good.

"Delicious!" I said. "What did you say it was made from?"

"Lentils," she said, shifting the baby to the other arm, obviously relieved that I had liked it. "They're little beans. You cook them until they're tender then moosh them. Then you mix them up with some taco spices. Add some bits of lettuce, green pepper and tomato, and put them on the crackers or taco shells."

"Cool!" I answered, licking away the cracker crumbs and any drool that might have escaped my mouth as I longed for more of those ugly, delicious cracker tacos.

But I didn't impose. Knowing I could eat up their entire supply before I'd get my fill, I moved on to have milk and granola at the beach, looking forward to the time I could cook my own. (*Thirty years later, I still love lentils tacos, and have great taco and taco salad recipes in this book.*)

As I drove away, trying to commit the word *lentils* to memory so I could buy some for myself, I felt that somehow it wasn't the first time I'd encountered that word. I seemed to recall that when I was in the bookstore looking at vegetarian cookbooks, I'd seen a couple of recipes calling for that strange word, *lentils*. Now that I knew what they were, I wished I'd bought that book. I wondered, could it be that those other strange-sounding ingredients might surprise me with such great tastes?

I was beginning to realize that the secret of becoming a happy vegetarian was to not be so reluctant. Maybe I needed to be willing to explore new things. If we're going to find cuisine treasure, apparently we gotta' take some chances.

Overcoming food prejudices

"But I don't have any food prejudices," you protest.

Humm. If you're like I was when I first became a vegetarian, you probably have more prejudices than you know. The *American Heritage Dictionary* defines prejudice as, as *an adverse judgment or opinion formed beforehand or without knowledge or examination of the facts,* and as *a preconceived preference or idea.* If my pre-vegetarian attitudes didn't meet those criteria, I don't know what would have. I'd had the unexamined, adverse opinion that a vegetarian diet was bland and lifeless, and that a decent meal was a plate with meat in the middle ringed with decorations consisting of salad, potatoes, and wimpy veggies to be eaten "because they're good for you."

It was only after beginning to examine my food assumptions that I learned how deep many of my prejudices ran.

For instance, when I was three years old my grandfather took me with him to help neighbors dig a well. The day was overcast and the hole they were digging by hand was deep and frightening, and the neighbor's home was dark and musty. The farmer's wife offered me a piece of rhubarb pie, which, feeling as overwhelmed as I did, I refused. For the next 30 years, unconsciously associating it with the memory of that day, I adamantly insisted that I didn't like rhubarb—even though the truth was that I had never tasted it. When I did try it (reluctantly of course) I liked it.

> ***Many adults have not reexamined their childhood belief that says,* "But I don't like vegetables."**

Likewise, many of our beliefs about food have been with us since childhood. As children we typically dislike vegetables. As adults, we shift into a new stage where we enjoy spicier, more complex foods, and are much more likely to enjoy the taste of veggies. But I've noticed that many adults have not reexamined their childhood belief that makes them say, *I don't like vegetables.* Also, my experience has been also that even people with long-standing beliefs that they dislike certain foods change their minds when they eat my vegetarian dishes.

For example ...

"What is this, tofu pudding?" a former boyfriend smirked, referring to the cauliflower-potato soup I had just served him. He hated cauliflower. I knew if I told this macho man what was in it, he would have refused to eat it ... on principal.

Jungle survival law says, if it smells good, eat it," I quipped. "Smells pretty good, doesn't it?"

He sniffed cautiously. "Yeah," he admitted reluctantly. Still not ready to give in, he grumbled, "But what's in it?"

"Don't ask yet, just taste it," I dared him.

"But I don't like eating something I don't know the name of," he continued to protest.

I didn't know if I wasn't going to win on this one or not. I made one last try. "Come on Sweetie Pie, give it a try and then I'll tell you, I promise."

Finally, he tried it. He had eaten a third of it before I admitted to him that it was half cauliflower. He continued to grumble resistively—but he ate the whole thing. The next time I served it, there wasn't even a peep of protest.

Like numerous other carnivores I've fed who claimed to dislike veggies, he eventually ate everything I fixed, including not only cauliflower but tofu, couscous, and other things he'd never even heard of before meeting me, foods that I myself had been prejudiced against when I first stopped eating meat. I've been amazed at how easy it is to convert someone to vegetarianism by simply serving great tasting food. And no one, in my thirty plus years of being a vegetarian, has ever asked, "But where's the beef?"

Getting Beyond the Belief that Vegetables are Boring

In overcoming my own prejudices, I had to begin by getting beyond a general disrespect for non-meat dishes. "Put some bacon in to given them some flavor," my grandparent's generation would say, as if that was the only way green beans could be made to have taste and character. The attitude many of us were raised with is that we're proud to be meat eaters because veggies are for wimps, mere side dishes for the meat and therefore inferior in worth, nutrition, or taste. What kind of beliefs did you or your family have about non-meat foods? Here are some common prejudices and concerns about vegetarianism.

Prejudice, Misconceptions	Examined Facts
• Vegetarianism is a starvation diet, i.e., "rabbit food."	• Vegetarians eat a wide variety of delicious, satisfying foods, and because natural tastes better, it's really gourmet everyday.
• Vegetarian recipes are made from strange, unfamiliar foods such as millet, tofu, and brown rice.	• True, many vegetarians become culinary explorers who eat foods that may be uncommon to meat eaters. If you wish, however, you can—with a little modification—still use your favorite cookbook. (BTW, there are no recipes in this book for brown rice—it's too hard to digest.)
• Vegetables are boring.	• Properly cooked veggies are delicious. But many people *think* they dislike vegetables because they remember disliking them as children, and because they have never had properly cooked vegetables. (But wait until you try my recipes.)

Prejudice, Misconception	Examined Facts
• It's hard to get enough protein on a vegetarian diet.	• Not true! Research shows that balanced vegetarian diets meet or exceed minimum daily requirements.
• Protein from vegetables is not as good as protein from meat.	• Protein is protein. In fact, nutrition from non-meat sources may be better because it comes in more digestible forms. Further, non-meat fresh foods are more likely to be free of chemicals, additives, and hormones.
• It's hard to get enough calcium and other nutrients on a vegetarian diet.	• The truth is, according to research studies, the absorption of calcium may be superior on a vegetarian diet.
• Vegetarians have less energy than meat eaters.	• Published studies show no appreciable differences between the fatigue index of vegetarians and non-vegetarians. Even some athletes are vegetarians.

Food prejudices can keep us stuck. Let's find out how to get unstuck

CHAPTER 3
Why Would Anyone in Her Right Mind Ever Become A Vegetarian?

"Try it and see for yourself."

Ah, the arrogance of youth. At the very moment I was wondering why anyone would want to be a vegetarian, millions of intelligent, practical people who were very much in their right minds were already enjoying the benefits. Here are reasons why they stopped eating meat, or never started.

Improved Health

- Vegetarians are generally healthier and live longer. Many doctors prescribe vegetarian diets to prevent or treat heart disease, cancer and other illness.
- On an vegetarian diet, we are not eating growth hormones, stimulants, antibiotics, and other chemicals used to feed or process meat.
- Vegetarians are rarely troubled with overweight.
- Vegetarians usually have sweeter breath and body odors. (Most nitrogen from excess protein comes out through sweat.)

According to a* Vegetarian Times *poll, nearly half of vegetarians switched to a non-meat diet for their health. The other half chose this diet style for reasons that included the influence of family and friends, to protect animals, or for ethical or environmental reasons. About a fifth of respondents said they didn't have intellectual reasons for becoming vegetarians; they just found themselves spontaneously choosing it.

Advantages for Animals and the Environment

- A vegetarian diet is easier on the environment. The primary reason for bulldozing the jungles (the world's greatest potential source of medicinal herbs) is to provide land for grazing for the meat industry. In case you wondered, it requires, on average, 55 square feet of land to produce a single meat patty.
- But not all bulldozing happens in the Amazon. In the U.S. alone more than 260 million acres of U.S. forest have been cleared in order to raise animals for eating. By switching to a vegetarian diet we each save approximately an acre of trees.
- An estimated 85 per cent of U.S. topsoil loss is directly associated with livestock raising.
- Livestock production consumes more than half of all water used for all purposes in the U.S., including nonrenewable underground sources.
- By being a vegetarian, we prevent the suffering of countless animals and birds in farm factories. Farm factories mass produce living beings—chickens, turkeys, cows, calves, pigs, piglets, and other animals—under heartbreakingly unnatural and overcrowded conditions. They're concentration camps for critters.
- Over the course of our lifetime, by not eating meat we will have saved the lives—*and the sufferings associated with their production for profit*—of approximately 1,000 animals.

Spiritual Values

- Historically, those seeking full development of human potential (enlightenment) have been advised to become vegetarians. On a no-meat diet we feel lighter and more awake inside, more attuned to our own body and its needs.
- Honoring and preserving life allows us to feel more intimate with nature.
- Not eating meat may strengthen our sense of worth, knowing that we make a contribution in eliminating violence.

Economic Benefits

- Food bills on meatless diets are less.
- This leaves more money to spend on other, more desirable kinds of foods, including those that might have been considered luxuries before.

Greater Happiness, Greater Pleasure

- Many vegetarians report that once they have eliminated the effects of meat from their diet, their taste buds seem to become more alive.
- Vegetarian cuisine is delicious.

How many people in the US are vegetarians?

Data gathered from a variety of polls typically show that between 20 and 25 percent of the U.S. population is interested in avoiding red meat. Between six and seven percent, or approximately 20 million Americans consider themselves vegetarians.

Of this number, approximately a million are vegan, meaning they take vegetarianism so seriously they eat no animal products at all, meaning no meat, fish, fowl, milk, dairy products, eggs or even honey.

Increasingly, scientific studies show that animal flesh isn't the best choice for human consumption. Meat is linked to cardiovascular disease, cancer, and numerous other tragic—and preventable—illnesses. In contrast, statistics show that eating vegetables and grains helps to *prevent* these same diseases and to increase longevity.

Among other health benefits, studies show that Vegetarians have lower rates of:

- Hypertension
- Overweight
- Cholesterol and other factors associated with reduced risk of coronary artery disease
- Some forms of cancer, such as colon, breast, prostrate and lung cancer
- Mortality from several chronic degenerative diseases
- Mortality in general
- Uric acid stone formation
- Diabetes Mellitus

The real question is, why would anyone in his or her right mind NOT want to become a vegetarian?

Well, of course ... it would be because they *didn't know how delicious vegetarian food is.*

Pizza!

CHAPTER 4
Acquiring New Tastes, Menus, & Sources of Nutrition

"My goodness, I didn't realize there were so many other options."

"I'd like to eat less meat but I don't know what else to fix." I bet I've heard that response a million times over the years when I told others I was a vegetarian.

At first I didn't know what to fix either. Like many other meat-eaters I found it hard to imagine what vegetarians ate and why they claimed it is so enjoyable. Like many of them, when I thought of a vegetarian meal, I imagined a plate of food with a gaping hole in the center where the meat was supposed to go, leaving nothing to eat but limp veggies and raw salads—mere *rabbit food.*

But vegetarianism is much more than a meat meal minus the meat; it's a move into a whole different world of food flavors and perspectives. Even though I'd learned a new recipe here and there, for the first couple of years after becoming a vegetarian, I was still holding the meat-meal-minus the meat mentality. It wasn't until I became a student at Maharishi University of Management in Fairfield Iowa that I really began to understand the difference between meat thinking and vegetarian thinking. As a vegetarian university with students from 50 different countries, the menu at MUM was widely varied to accommodate tastes from different cultures—and so delicious I was always eager to get to the next meal. After graduating, I ended up working on volunteer staff for a year, from prep to cook to dining hall manager. That was when I finally began to understand from behind the scenes about nutrition and menu planning ... and to become so enthusiastic about vegetarian food that I began to experiment on my own. In the woods, when I thought I was going to have give up all my favorite meat dishes, I thought it was going to be a terrible loss. But by the time I had become a cook in a vegetarian kitchen, I knew absolutely that what at first looks like a loss often turns out in the end to be a gain. Given enough experience, I bet you will feel the same way.

Enlivening your taste buds as a culinary explorer

Inundated as we are with microwaved, processed, canned, frozen and fast foods, many of us have turned off our taste buds. Many have become so habituated to frozen dinners, fast food restaurants, and snack foods that these are the tastes they crave, in part because they don't know there are better alternatives. "Hey, let's go get a burger at McDonalds," or "You know, I really have a hankering for (brand name) meatloaf dinner."

Organic vs. Conventional Supermarket Food

I used to think the hullabaloo about organic foods was silly. Why not simply wash the produce to get rid of pesticides and fertilizers?

Then I began to get it, that the problem was more than skin deep. Produce "eats" from the soil around it so pesticides and fertilizers are inside and **we eat them.**

Besides being chemical-free, organic food tastes better and is higher in nutrition. For instance, if you still eat meat, then compare organic to chemical-fed factory-farmed chicken. The flesh of the organic chicken is pink, tender and plush, while the non-organic chicken meat is dry, whitish, and tough. Likewise, oversized chemical veggies often taste like cardboard while organic veggies taste juicy and alive. Given a choice, even animals will chose organic over conventional.

Most important of all, organic also means it's **safe from genetic tampering.** *Many of our foods are now genetically modified to give them a longer shelf life, make them more tolerant of cold, more resistant to bugs*—**and to make them better able to withstand heavier doses of fertilizers and pesticides.**

Genetically modified (GM) foods are not required to be labeled, so unless it's organic, food may contain anything. It may look like a tomato but if it has insect genes in it, it's actually a tomaskito, and no one knows the long-term outcome of eating such "Frankenfoods" or the long-term effects of genetic drift as GM seeds are eaten by wildlife or mingled with healthy crops. We do know at the very least that in eating GM foods we're eating heavier doses of fertilizers and pesticides. The **only** *way to keep from being used as a guinea pig in a huge genetic experiment is to eat foods labeled* **organic.**

But have you noticed that fast foods, frozen dinners, and prepared sandwiches or pizza that has been cooked all day at the local EAT GAS quick mart or in the office vending machines generally taste like cardboard? Do you find yourself thinking, "Well, at least it's quick," so you pretend to not notice how dull and dead the taste is? Ignoring our taste buds is like deadening our emotions, and chances are, you think the fatigued, bloated, or dulled-out feelings after eating is just normal.

But, on a vegetarian diet we begin to wake up and discover ourselves feeling more energetic and more mentally alert. Just as it happened for me in the woods, it dawns on us that *what we eat has a powerful effect on both body and mind.* Then we also just naturally begin to "get it," that the fresher the food, the better it tastes and the better we feel after eating. Remember the cook at the Bo Tree? "Fresh," he'd said. "Begin with the freshest ingredients." The reason he said that is because he knew what we discover when we eat a fresh diet—that *fresh tastes better* and it leaves us feeling better.

On a vegetarian diet, we also begin to discover that we feel better if we eat *whole* foods. Whole food is just what it says, the whole thing, just as nature made it, naturally balanced within itself. It is food the body recognizes and processes *as* food. Partial ingredients, on the other hand, are some sliced-off aspect that the body may actually believe is a foreign substance—a possible cause for allergies. For instance, naturally occurring fiber foods lowers cholesterol and has other benefits, but *isolated* fiber (listed as "maltodextrin," "polydextrose," or "inulin) is just trash. Along with artificial flavors, vitamins, etc., what you get is a screaming sort of deliciousness with little true nutrition.

> ***Just as happened to me in the woods, it dawns on us that* what we eat has a powerful effect on both body and mind.**

Another problem with artificial ingredients is that they disguise real taste. For instance, did you know that dog food (which is made up of all kinds of scrap ingredients) is so processed that in order to have taste it must be sprayed with flavored oils? Chances are we would be disgusted by many processed foods for humans if we actually understood what was in them and how they were made. Taste is our body's first signal in recognizing what is good for it to eat, so it is important that we not try to fool it. Once we begin regularly eating natural, chemical -free food, we begin to like this honest taste, even crave it the way we once craved chemical-laden stuff.

So, shift happens. It may not happen overnight, but because whole, natural foods taste better and leave us feeling better after we eat them, we just naturally find ourselves wanting to eat a higher quality of foods. Because of this shift, our taste preferences naturally begin to change.

Becoming a Culinary Explorer

If you're like me when I first began, you may be reluctant to try new tastes or to give up old favorites. But the good news is, tastes are mostly acquired. For example, our taste changes naturally as we grow older. Our tastes also change naturally with new experience and with long time experience. We can learn to like anything. Fortunately, it's easy to learn to like good, healthy food.

Sure, some people enjoy being disdainful connoisseurs when something doesn't perfectly suit their palate. For them, I offer the old saying that *he who is hard to please is hardly ever pleased.*

For myself, I'd rather find every bit of pleasure in life that I can. So rather than be limited to a narrow range of favorites (most families alternate an average of only ten recipes), after becoming a vegetarian I became determined to try to enjoy as many types and styles of food as possible. To avoid getting trapped in the same old taste habits, I use my mother's "three times" rule of tongue. This means, try new foods at least three times. But even if you don't like it after the third time, why not stay willing to revisit it later?

Ways to Learn New Tastes

- *Eat at a good vegetarian restaurant. How will you know if it's a good restaurant? Because the food will taste great.*
- *If you have vegetarian friends, wrangle an invitation to eat at their table, or at least ask for favorite recipes.*
- *Try vegetarian cookbooks. Your local library or bookstore has many books available on vegetarian cuisine and menu planning.*
- *Get advice from those at your local farm market, orchard market, CSA or health food store.*
- *Look up "vegetarian" on the Internet. It's loaded with websites that offer advice, suggestions for substitutes, and free recipes. (such as my sister site, www.reluctant veggies.com)*
- *Experiment in your own kitchen.*
- *Try my recipes!*

Pushing the taste envelope

As a young adult, I detested bell peppers. Why anyone thought they were tasty enough to be used for anything but compost was a mystery to me. But one day it occurred to me to wonder, "What does green pepper taste like to someone who loves it?"

To find out, I pretended I'd never tasted it before, then bit into one. The result was astonishing. The tangy, juicy taste filled my mouth with a zingy crispy freshness that I instantly fell in love with. I now use peppers as a staple in many of my favorite dishes, and even pack them in picnics to eat like apples. Needless to say, had I clung to my former prejudice, I would have missed a lot of great taste satisfaction.

Using this same method (of approaching foods as if I had never tasted them before) I was even successful in learning to enjoy many foods I thought I detested. For example, as a child and young adult, I found cottage cheese revolting. Can you imagine how I felt when, after falling in love with my college cafeteria's lasagna, I learned that the white stuff in it was ... you guessed it ... cottage cheese. *When I didn't know it was a food I disliked, I loved it.* Later, I challenged myself to learn to love cottage cheese without the disguise. It took a lot of courage to take my first few bites of that icky white stuff, but I succeeded and...you guessed it again... it became another pleasurable food (especially when mixed with pineapple and sunflower seeds).

Vegetarian Nutrition and Menu Planning

Okay (you may be admitting), maybe I do need to be a little more open in trying new tastes, but what about vegetarian nutrition? How will I know if I'm getting a balanced diet?

Good question. Remember how afraid I was that I might die of starvation on a two-week trip with no meat? After more than three decades of eating vegetarian I can laugh now. But I certainly didn't know then that even though vegetarian thinking is quite different from meat thinking, vegetarian nutrition and menu planning are not hugely different from meat nutrition and menu planning. Let me explain.

Awakening Your Taste Buds

Begin awakening your taste buds by becoming more conscious of what you eat. Use all five senses.

- **Look** ***at your food. Notice the colors, the visual texture, and the appearance on the plate. Does it appeal to your eyes? Great chefs know that visual presentation is of major importance. As anyone who has been on a cruise ship or other place where food is visually appealing can tell us, the sight of food is almost as important as aroma and taste.***

- **Savor** *the smells. What does your nose tell you about this food? Jungle survival law to determine if food is safe says simply,* **if it smells good, eat it.** *Beyond safety, aroma beckons us seductively. To anyone who loses the sense of smell, food tastes like cardboard. Give your nose an opportunity to enjoy. It is the gateway to the taste buds.*
- **Taste** *the food consciously. Take a bite, roll it around on your tongue, and let your taste buds explore the subtleties.*
- **Feel** *the textures as you bite and chew.*
- **Listen** *as you bite. Crunch (or lack of it) will alert you whether the food fresh or stale.* **Fresh foods, like those you find at your farm or orchard market, or have delivered from your local Community Organized Agriculture (CSA), are always more full of life than foods that are canned, frozen, or trucked all the way across the country.**

As a vegetarian, where will I get my protein?

Vegetarians get their protein from dairy products (milk, yogurt, cheese, eggs), from legumes (beans and peas), grains (wheat, corn, rice, etc.), nuts and seeds, and to some degree from most other foods.

How will I know if I'm getting enough protein?

Frances Moore Lappe, author of *Diet for a Small Planet,* who popularized the idea of combining foods to produce whole proteins, later retracted that idea, saying that in all but the most extreme diets, *"If people are getting enough calories, they are virtually certain of getting enough protein."* In fact, research says that Americans typically eat almost twice as much protein as their bodies require (placing unnecessary strain on the liver) and studies show that even vegetarians can eat too much protein.

Rules of Tongue for a Balanced Diet

The simplest rules of nutrition can be summed up in five words: **fresh, organic, variety, contrast, and balance.**

But how can I really be certain I'm getting enough nutrition?

After discovering for themselves that what we eat affects the way we feel, some vegetarians become obsessed with nutrition. That's fine if that's your thing, but that wasn't for me. I didn't want to spend time calculating what has vitamin this or vitamin that; I just wanted to enjoy the food. Surely, I thought, humankind wouldn't have survived umpteen hundreds of thousand of years if we needed a textbook to figure out what to eat. What has worked for me is what I call the color theory Rule of Tongue for getting proper nutrition: I eat some green stuff and some red stuff and some brown stuff and some white stuff and then some different green stuff. I pick out a main-dish recipe that's high in protein (more on this in following chapters), add a grain or starch and add a veggie or two on the side, just the same as in creating meat menus. I use whole, natural, fresh foods, all preferably organic. I eat some cooked foods and some raw foods. I eat some crunchy stuff and some creamy stuff. If you eat different foods from one meal to the next, create a pretty plate of high-quality food with a variety of colors and textures, how could you miss not getting enough nutrition?

How do I learn Vegetarian Menu Planning?

No problem. Just do the same thing you did when you planned a meat menu—pick a protein dish, add a starch like rice or potatoes, add some cooked veggies, and something raw. Easy, huh?

Speaking of raw, is it better to eat foods raw or cooked?

Some people believe that diets high in raw foods are best, but others believe that cooked is more digestible. My recommendation: eat some of both, at least until you are more familiar with what your individual body needs. Balance is the key to good health.

What if I want to be on the safe side and combine proteins?

If Lappe is right, it isn't necessary but if you want to do it, it's easy. First of all, nature has given us a built-in intuition, which, if we haven't buried it under mounds of intellectual do's and don'ts, pushes us toward proper nutrition. For instance, our ancestors had no nutritionists to guide them, yet many recipes and menus handed down to us automatically combine the right foods for complete proteins: beans and cornbread, beans and tortillas, beans and rice, milk and potatoes, macaroni and cheese and so forth. Here again we encounter ancient wisdom in practical action. Cravings are either signals that your body needs that thing you crave, or a sign of old bad habits. Learn to distinguish and then trust your food intuition. Studies show that children who are allowed to pick their own diets will, after a period of bingeing on the sweet stuff, naturally begin to pick a more balanced diet.

Rules of Tongue for Combining Proteins

This rule is simple. When you serve beans, serve a grain also. Or if you serve a grain, serve nuts and seeds or dairy. That's all there is to it.

Here's a chart for combining protein. Don't feel you need to carry it around with you, worried that you aren't combining foods correctly to get necessary nutrition.

Rules of Tongue for Combining Plant Proteins

To get all eight amino acids, serve any item in Column I with any item in Column II, or serve any item in column II with any item in Column III.

I	II	III
Legumes (Beans and Peas)	**Grains**	**Seeds and Nuts**
black beans	barley	almonds
kidney beans	bulgar	cashews
red beans	corn	coconut
pink beans	oats	pecans
pinto beans	rice	pine nuts
navy beans	rye	pistachios
mung beans	trilicale	pumpkin seeds
lima beans	wheat	sesame seeds
black-eyed peas	pasta	sunflower seeds
lentils		
soybeans		
green or yellow peas		
garbanzos (chickpeas)		

Note: tofu contains all eight amino acids.

Other major sources of protein include milk, cheese and eggs.

Okay, so maybe now you're a little less reluctant, are you ready to ask how to make the transition?

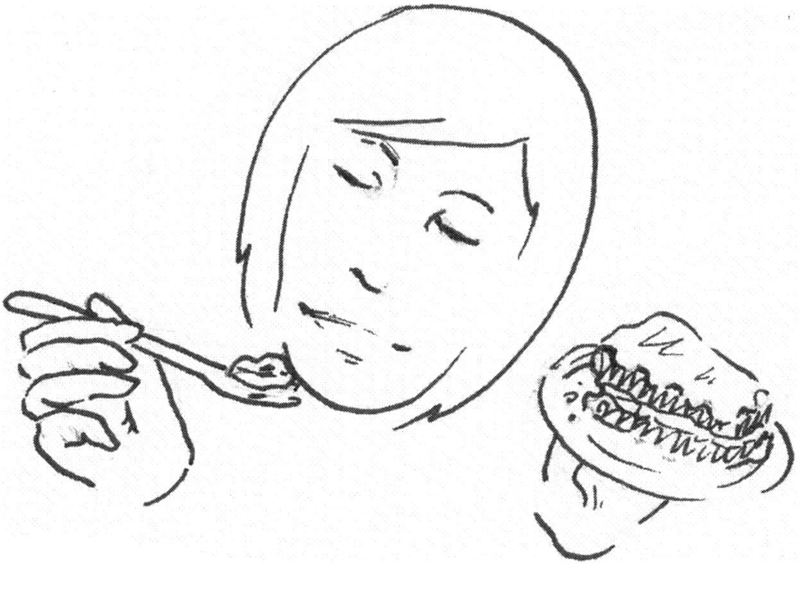

CHAPTER 5
Discovering Veggies

"But I Don't Like Vegetables."

Not like vegetables? Excuse me if I chuckle. I thought I didn't like vegetables either until after I became a vegetarian and discovered my negative opinion had been based on what I *thought* of as vegetables—poorly cooked, essentially lifeless stuff probably picked weeks, possibly even years earlier by a machine and then canned or otherwise processed. Yuck.

My dislike for vegetables was also based on being raised with a prejudice against non-meat foods. How many times have you heard someone claim, proudly, "I'm a meat-and-potatoes person; I never eat vegetables." I've been one of those. Mom may have said, "Eat your vegetables—they're good for you," but she and other relatives also said things like, "Oh, yes, we need a vegetable so how about if we add some buttered peas?" Or ,"We need some color for the meat and potatoes, shall we put some corn on the side?" Or, "How about adding bacon into the green beans to give them some flavor?"

The not-so-subtle message was that vegetables are not only less important or nutritious than meat, but that they are in fact merely afterthoughts or garnishes for the *respectable* part of the meal—the meat. The importance of vegetables was deemphasized further because, let's face it, canned, frozen, microwaved or leftover vegetables are boring. That kind of taste is enough to make anyone reluctant to be a vegetarian.

However, such soggy, tasteless, limp vegetables are not what vegetarians eat. Had I known, on the day I so arrogantly said to myself that vegetarians couldn't possibly be in their right minds, just how mouth-watering delicious meatless food really is, I wouldn't have waited to get started becoming one.

Even though I stopped eating meat overnight, the taste transition didn't happen that fast. It took a little while to adjust. But the more I learned, the more I realized that vegetarian thinking was larger and more diverse than meat thinking. Plus, after a little time to actually try it, I found greater taste satisfaction as a vegetarian—as well discovering an interesting variety that assured me that I had made the right choice. I'm willing to bet that you will like it better too.

Discovering A Love of Vegetables

Research says that there are stages of tastes as we grow from childhood to old age. In childhood the taste we like best is sweet, and the taste we like *least* is, you guessed it, vegetables. I think a lot of us get stuck in the memory of disliking vegetables, so as adults, when we're more apt to like the taste, we don't give them a fair chance to impress us.

To overcome childhood prejudice and to awaken your taste buds, begin by experiencing vegetables as if for the first time. Forget all your preconceptions and pretend you've never seen or tasted them before Sure, I know it sounds silly but what do you have to lose? I can almost guarantee that you'll discover that you have been eating on "automatic pilot" and that experiencing food from a more awake perspective is a real taste-bud opener.

Step One: Experiences Vegetables in each stage of preparation from raw to cooked

Begin with vegetables in their most natural state—raw and fresh. Sadly, many people have never eaten foods farm fresh so they don't know that there's a huge difference between the one or two week-old vegetables in the supermarket and that same vegetable picked straight off the vine or fresh from the orchard perhaps only hours earlier.

To get the freshest foods to experiment with, go to a farm or orchard market, or find a farmer who delivers fresh produce to you on a weekly basis (CSA). Also check out for yourself the vast taste difference between organic and non-organic. If your only source of food is a regular grocery store, then at least look for vegetables that are crisp and firm.

Whatever the source, pick a veggie you find the most appealing to look at. After scrubbing it squeaky clean, give it your full attention. Look at it as if this was the first time you've ever seen this vegetable. (For some folks it may actually be the first time you've seen it, or eaten it, or even knew the name of it. The general public is so undereducated about fresh foods that checkers at the grocery stores often have to ask me the name of the vegetable they are trying to ring up on the register.)

The average stalk of fresh broccoli (including the stems) contains 35 percent USDA minimum daily requirements of vitamin A, 32 percent of B vitamins, 20 percent of vitamin C, 25 percent folic acid, etc.—all at only 50 calories

Now look at it as if there's a secret gift inside, if only you can find the mystery key to unlock it. Roll it in your hands, feel, smell, and look, even listen (a psychic I know claims that veggies sing). Marvel at what grows out of the ground for you...crisp, blue-green broccoli, mellow-yellow squash, zing-green zucchini, velvet-black eggplant.

Now, ask yourself, what is it that a lover of this vegetable tastes? Then bite into it.

Slowly, consciously, taste it. Distinguish its texture on your tongue; is it crunchy, soft, crisp, smooth or rough? Is it dry or full of juice, tart or sweet? Let curiosity about its character inspire you to ask questions such as, would it taste good in a dip tray or salad, or is there a rawness or hardness to it that might taste better cooked and maybe "married" with other foods?

Step Two: Experienced Plain Cooked Veggies Anew

The next step is to try it cooked. To get acquainted with its true flavor, the first time you try to understand veggies from this "new" perspective, use no seasonings. I suggest you also try cooking to various degrees of doneness to compare the tastes. For instance, you may love the crisp, snappy taste of raw asparagus, or find its distinctive flavor better when cooked to crisp-tender. Or you may find the opposite, that it tastes better to you when it is thoroughly cooked. But one thing is for sure; each thing you learn about vegetables will make you a better cook and a better consumer.

Step Three: Experiment with New Ways to Prepare Veggies

You probably have some long-standing recipes or habitual ways of cooking vegetables, and these make feel you already know how it should taste. But flavors change with each style of cooking—steaming, boiling, frying, baking, broiling—and food tastes are influenced by other foods cooked with them. You may find vegetables you disliked served alone actually taste great in casseroles or other recipes where they meld with other flavors and textures.

Step Four: Experiment with Herbs and Spices, Sauces and Gravies, Mixes, and Combinations

You also might find that you like veggies cooked one way but not another. For instance, you may not enjoy the texture or taste of steamed okra, but when it is prepared in a spicy Creole gumbo, you may love it.

Step Five: Try Veggies cooked in ways you never thought of before

With an attitude of discovery, you'll find many surprises in store. For instance, you already know that pumpkin is wonderful in pies or breads. But did you know that it also makes a delicious, creamy soup? Did you know that cinnamon tastes great on broccoli? Had it ever occurred to you to put nuts on spaghetti? Be prepared to try new things that don't immediately fit with your habitual way of thinking about food.

Discovering that Mother was right—vegetables are good for you

As a child I often wondered why Mom could claim that anything that tasted so awful—vegetables—could be good for me. As it turns out, Mom and I were both right. According to ancient wisdom, deliciousness is important as an aid to happy, healthy digestion. But other than new potatoes, tomatoes, green beans and summer time corn-on-the cob, we almost never had fresh veggies, and let's face it, if it's not fresh, it's *not* delicious. Fresh is wonderful. Besides having a lively taste when properly prepared, fresh vegetables are jam-packed with nutrients. For instance, the average stalk of fresh broccoli (including the stems) contains 35 percent USDA minimum daily requirements of vitamin A, 32 percent of B vitamins, 20 percent of vitamin C, 25 percent folic acid, etc.—all at only 50 calories.

Eating fresh vegetables has many positive side benefits. Studies show, for instance, that a high fiber diet from vegetables is a natural cancer preventative and has other important health, weight, and longevity benefits. This alone makes it well worth a try to cultivate a taste for veggies, wouldn't you agree?

CHAPTER 6
Making the Transition

"Now that I'm not so reluctant, how do I become a vegetarian?"

Once convinced it's the right thing to do, some people make the transition all at once, as I did, then bungle to find a way through it. Others do so more gradually, beginning with a few non-meat dishes a week. Either way, chances are you'll not only survive but thrive.

Do I Have To Give Up All My Favorite Foods?

No. You'll probably find that over time old favorites get replaced with new favorites, and that by using the recipes for meat substitutes in my book (or buying substitutes pre-made), you may find it satisfies quite nicely to use them in your favorite recipes in place of the meat. Often it isn't the meat so much as the flavorings that give a dish its unique taste.

Different Levels of Vegetarianism

You also might also want to experiment with different levels of vegetarianism.

The different Levels of Vegetarianism

Semi-Vegetarian: *some people cut out the red meat while still willing to eat seafood and poultry. At least there is less cholesterol and animal fat in skinned poultry and seafood. To avoid the chemicals, choose only free range organic.*

Oro-lacto Vegetarian: *Oro-lacto vegetarians will eat dairy products including milk, cheese, and eggs, but as one vegetarian put it, "I will not eat anything with a face."*

Lacto-Vegetarian: *Lacto-vegetarians use milk and other dairy products but do not eat eggs or any kind of meat.*

Vegan: *Vegans not only don't eat flesh, they don't eat animal product of any kind, and do not wear animal products such as leather.*

It's a funny thing, but the more intensely restricted one defines one's level of diet, the more seriously one tends to think that is the only level that is the correct one. My opinion is, the right way is what works for you. With great respect for those who believe we shouldn't eat animal products of any kind, it is also my opinion that jumping into veganism is probably too extreme for a new vegetarian. Keep an open mind and let your body tell you what to eat.

Avoid Crash Changes and Radical Diets

To begin, you might want to simply try a few vegetarian meals a week, maybe getting the rest of the family involved in exploring this new diet style. Thumb through this or other vegetarian cookbooks and see what might appeal to you. Chances are, you'll find unfamiliar ingredients and the recipes may seem pretty strange at first. But here's the trick to good eating: *try* those unfamiliar foods. Remember, this is an adventure and your mission is to discover new tastes.

Get advice from the folks at your local farm market, orchard, CSA, or health food store.

I used to avoid health food stores, feeling that going to such places was for sissies and eccentrics. But this was another useless prejudice.

"In the early days of our business we had mostly young people," says a successful health food store owner, "but now everybody comes in—young, old, students, housewives, ethnic groups, and apparently there are a lot of working people because Saturday is our best day." Many mainstream grocery stores have become aware of the growing demand and now carry items that used to be found only in specialty stores, including such foods as organic dairy products and vegetables, tofu, black beans, basmati rice, couscous and many other vegetarian favorites. Even so, foods are almost always fresher at your local farm markets, CSA's, co-ops, and health food stores. These are good places to get advice, find new information, and discover alternatives for meat, eggs, and milk. Most importantly, these are places to get fresh, whole, unprocessed ORGANIC foods that you may not find anywhere else.

Meat- and Dairy-Alternatives

While you are learning to enjoy vegetarianism, there are a number of meat-like substitutes that may make the transition easier. For instance, it is increasingly easy to find good-tasting vegetarian alternatives for sausage, bacon, chicken, burgers, hot dogs, and pepperoni. I encourage you to move away from packaged foods but if you like the taste of packaged meals such as Hamburger Helper or Chicken Delight, then continue to use these but substitute tofu, tofu hamburger (page 73), or TVP (Textured Vegetable Protein)—made from soy products, which are available in almost any health food store.

For those of you who choose to stop eating red meat but don't want a radical change to a completely non-meat diet, you will find frozen turkey-burgers, turkey or chicken ham, bologna, and hot-dogs. Also, if you miss the chewy fiber of red meat, well-cooked duck has a similar hearty meat flavor and texture.

If you do not wish to eat any meat at all yet still crave meat flavor and texture, my original tofu hamburger recipes starting on page 73 should help. You may also enjoy the recipes for gluten "meats" in the book *How to Make All the Meat You Eat Out of Wheat* by Nina and Michael Shandler. If you don't want to eat any meat but miss the "chewiness," nut *meats* and seeds may satisfy.

Substitutes for eggs and milk are abundant, both in health foods stores and supermarkets. Substitutes for cow's milk include soy, rice and nut milk. (Also see the breakfast section of this cookbook for more ideas.) You can also add meaty flavor with homemade or store-bought broths and soups, bouillon cubes, and vegetable/herb combinations. Some of these contain meat, so if you want to eliminate all meat, be sure to read labels.

How To Tell Others That You Are A Vegetarian

I became a vegetarian in the early seventies when the mainstream considered vegetarianism to be radical, even unhealthy. But in today's health-conscious society, many people appear to feel envious that someone has made the transition to a healthier diet style. Now, simply saying, "I'm a vegetarian," or "I don't eat meat," may actually earn you some respect. If it happens that anyone thinks you're weird, just laugh to yourself and remember my arrogant belief that no one in his right mind would choose vegetarianism ... only to shortly afterward become a vegetarian and eventually write a book about it. With the right experience, they just might change their minds too.

How to be a Vegetarian and Eat in Non-Vegetarian Places

If I'm invited out to dinner in a non-vegetarian's home, I generally politely explain ahead of time that I'm a vegetarian. I may ask if they'd like me to contribute a vegetarian dish or, to avoid stress and concerns at family gatherings, I'll tell them I'd be comfortable eating fish and poultry should they choose to serve these in place of red meat. If the menu can't be changed, then sometimes I eat ahead of time or simply eat extra veggies.

To eat Aunt Myrtle's spaghetti or not...

It frequently happens that as we experience the benefits of being a vegetarian, we develop a strong aversion to eating meat in any form. Even poultry and fish may seem heavy and dulling. However, in the context of an overall healthy diet and generally good digestion, the atmosphere in which food is eaten is at least as important as what we eat. If you find yourself in a situation where you are served meat and you cannot courteously refuse or surreptitiously dispose of it, then simply say "Thank you," bless the cook, and continue to enjoy the food and the company. You can always fast later.

Eating out

Better restaurants always have vegetarian options, and you can almost always find non-meat foods at Italian and Oriental restaurants. Otherwise, there is a range of possibilities. McDonald's reports that some vegetarians simply ask for sandwiches without the meat, meaning they have a lettuce, tomato and dressing sandwich, or they ask for cheeseburgers without the meat. Burger King offers a vegetarian sandwich. Increasingly, restaurants such as Ruby Tuesdays and TGI Fridays offer vegetarian entrees and sandwiches.

Many menu items have vegetarian substitutes. For instance, you can almost always request that beans be substituted for meat in Mexican food—bean tacos, bean tostados, and so forth. Some restaurants will substitute vegetables or grain dishes in place of meat.

Vegetarian meals are also available on airlines if you call well in advance. They need 36 to 48 hours notice.

Fortunately, the world is becoming more health conscious, and since demand is what creates supply, your becoming a vegetarian helps to create the demand that will someday fill the world with good vegetarian places to eat.

Last and Most Important Piece of Advice: Keep your tummy happy.

Your tummy—and consequently your whole being—will be happier if you follow some simple, commonsense advice such as the Ayurvedic recommendation to, "Eat the foods you love *and that make you feel good afterwards.*" You may love the taste of meat, and you may not feel better after just one or two vegetarian meals, but the majority of us find that after a few days or weeks of a completely vegetarian diet, we recognize a distinct difference between how we feel after eating only vegetarian food compared to how we feel after eating meat. If you give your body a chance to purify out the chemicals and other residues from eating meat (at least two weeks), it will help you to see the difference. During that time, you may experience cravings for meat and possibly even some discomfort as your body purifies, but once past this stage, it is very likely that you will feel better and can begin being more sensitive to your body's needs.

While you are cultivating your intuition about what is best for you, you can use the dietary recommendations formulated by Edith Young Cottrell, a Loma Linda University research nutritionist. These recommendations are rediscovered age after age, and might well be a summary of advice that has lasted 60 centuries from the ancient alternative health care system, *Ayurveda.* Apply these laws below, taken from *The Oats, Peas, Beans & Barley Cookbook,* and you will live long and prosper.

Universal Advice for Good Health

- Drink freely of fresh, pure water.
- Eat wholesome foods.
- Eat simply.
- Eat moderately.
- Eat only at mealtimes.
- Eat slowly with thorough mastication.
- Provide fixed times of rest for the stomach.
- Take individual considerations (such as whether you are a child or adult, healthy or ill, having a strong or weak digestion, and type of work you do) into consideration in determining what kind of food you eat.
- Do not eat when emotionally upset.

Congratulations

Congratulations for having the courage to try a new diet style, and for making the positive health changes that will very likely extend the length of time in which your children will get to enjoy your company. Now go forth and experiment!

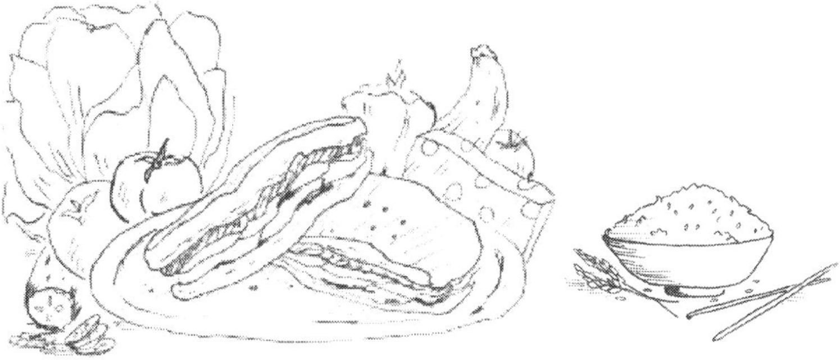

PART II
Recipes

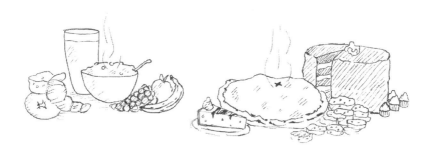

CHAPTER 7
Sources of Protein: Tofu

What Chinese call "Meat Without Bones"
and "the Joy of the Kitchen"

Vegetarians eat many things other than tofu, but I wanted to begin the recipe section by giving you an overview about why we like it, and because the next chapter is about how to make meat-tasting substitutes from it that may satisfy cravings for meat.

The first time I tasted tofu I was totally prepared to dislike it. What I found was that while it was as bland-tasting as it looked, it wasn't bad.

Yet the funny thing was, after eating it my body felt great. So, I tried it again. Same experience—I felt good after eating it. I've had this same experience with other high-nutrition foods I didn't immediately like (such as seaweed) but found that I quickly developed a taste for it because it was so deeply satisfying.

Later, after discovering how versatile tofu was in the kitchen, I became downright enthusiastic about this odd-looking cuisine. Made from boiling soybeans into a curd-like substance, its Chinese creators called tofu, "Yellow Jewel" and "Meat without Bones." It has some remarkable properties.

- Tofu is 95 percent digestible.
- It has the lowest ratio of calories to protein found in any known plant food. (1 gram of usable protein = 12 calories.)
- It contains all eight of the essential amino acids.
- Combined with grains, seeds, nuts, or dairy can increase the amount of available protein by as much as 40 percent.
- It has a high vitamin and mineral content. For instance, a 4-ounce serving contains 20 percent of the adult RDA for iron.
- It has a balanced alkaline-acidic factor.
- Unlike other beans, tofu contains virtually no starch.
- It's salt-free.
- It's cholesterol-free.
- In its organic form, it has no hormones or antibiotics and is free from pesticides and genetic tampering.
- Tofu has unmatched versatility in the kitchen; it can be prepared in an infinite number of recipes.

"Tofu? I'm surprised ... this tastes so great."

Because their experience with tofu has usually been limited to strips or chunks in stir-fries, Westerners usually believe tofu is bland and uninteresting. The truth is it has such a wide range of tastes and textures that it can be the "stuff" of creativity in the kitchen. It can be made as smooth as pudding or as fibrous as meat. In fact, you can do anything with it that you can do with meat: fry, steam, smoke, marinate, ferment, or make it into soups. It can be used for sauces, gravies, and creams. Speaking of cream, it is even made into 50 or so different varieties of ice cream. Being neutral in taste, it will also accept the flavor of whatever foods or spices it is cooked with. To make tofu taste like meat, freeze it solidly then thaw and wring out excess water before cooking. (More on this in the following chapter.)

Hint for cooking with tofu for yourself or family members who claim to dislike it:

My experience has been that if I cut tofu into small bits and season well before stirring it into a dish, many of those who dine with me don't recognize that tofu is even an ingredient.

If they don't ask, I don't tell. I just accept the compliments with a gracious smile.

Grilled Italian Tofu Kabobs

½ pound tofu: freeze tofu for at least 24 hours then thaw, wring out excess water and cut into 1 inch cubes
1 small eggplant, about 8 ounces, peeled and cut into 1 inch cubes
2 small fresh ripe tomatoes, quartered, or use cherry tomatoes
1 medium size zucchini, cut into 1-inch cubes
1 medium size yellow squash, cut into 1-inch cubes
1 green pepper, cut into 1-inch chunks
Optional: apples, sliced; pineapple, cubed

Italian Marinade for Kabobs

1 teaspoon basil
1 teaspoon thyme
¼ teaspoon black pepper
¼ cup soy sauce
1 tablespoon lemon juice
¼ cup olive oil
½ cup water

Soak vegetables and fruits in marinade overnight, and then place on a skewer. Wrap the kabobs in aluminum foil (or if you'd prefer not using aluminum, use an oiled stainless steel baking pan) and broil in outdoor grill or oven grill for 20 to 30 minutes. Uncover to brown last five minutes.

Tofu Veggie Pie

1 pound tofu, drained and cubed
2 medium potatoes, cubed small
2 medium carrots, sliced
½ head small cauliflower, broken into florets
2 stalks celery, sliced
1 cup frozen peas
2 tablespoons butter
1 teaspoon rosemary
½ teaspoon thyme
salt and pepper to taste

Sauté tofu in spices and butter. Parboil or steam vegetables until half tender. Mix together and spread in greased 13 x 9 baking pan.

Make a cream sauce using 4 teaspoons butter, 2 tablespoons flour, 2 cups milk, and ½ teaspoon parsley. Pour over vegetables and tofu mixture until covered. Spread with bread crumbs tossed in 2 teaspoons butter, ½ teaspoon basil, ¼ teaspoon savory and ¼ teaspoon salt. Bake at 350° for 1 hour.

Tofu "Chicken" and Fettuccine

8 ounces fettuccine noodles
2 tablespoons olive oil
½ pound fresh or frozen (thawed) tofu, well drained and cut into ½ inch cubes or strips
1 bell pepper, cut into matchstick strips, about 1 cup.
½ yellow bell pepper, cut into matchstick strips
¾ cup heavy cream

⅓ cup freshly grated Parmesan cheese
2 cups steamed broccoli
optional; coarsely grated lemon peel

Prepare fettuccine according to package directions. Fry tofu strips in oil until slightly brown. Remove from heat to drain. Add peppers to hot oil, cook until crisp-tender. Add cream, bring to a boil, reduce heat to medium and simmer 2 minutes, stirring to blend. Stir in grated Parmesan. Drain pasta and stir into vegetables. Serve garnished with broccoli tossed with grated lemon peel.

Tofu Stir-Fries

⅓ head of broccoli, cut or broken into florets
3 carrots, sliced thin
2 stalks celery, sliced
1 green pepper, cut into thin slices
¼ head of cabbage, cut into 1-inch squares
1 pound fresh or frozen (and thawed) tofu, well drained, diced
1 can sliced water chestnuts or bamboo, drained
½ cup sunflower seeds
1 teaspoon cinnamon
½ teaspoon grated fresh ginger

Place broccoli in hot skillet or wok with small amount of oil. Sprinkle cinnamon over broccoli. Stir constantly to prevent burning, for 3 to 4 minutes. Remove. Add carrots. Sprinkle carrots with ginger and fry for 3 to 4 minutes, stirring frequently. Add all the vegetables, with oil as needed to prevent sticking, stirring frequently to prevent scorching. Stir-fry sunflower seeds. Add 1 tablespoon of soy sauce to tofu and stir-fry. Mix all ingredients together and serve with rice and sweet-and-sour sauce. (See page 214 for recipe.)

Sharalyn Pliler

Avocado/Tofu Casserole

½ pound tofu
1 large ripe avocado
2 cups cottage cheese or mixture of cottage cheese and sour cream
2 cups cooked rice
1 tomato, cubed
1 teaspoon salt
¼ teaspoon pepper

Blend tofu, avocado and spices in the blender until smooth. Mix with cottage cheese, rice, and vegetables and pour into greased 9-inch baking dish. Bake at 375°F for 45 minutes.

Tofu Potatoes with Yogurt and Herbs

½ pound fresh tofu, drained
3 medium potatoes, boiled
2 tablespoons butter
⅔ cup unflavored yogurt
6 tablespoons chopped mixed herbs: parsley, dill, chervil
salt and pepper to taste

Purée tofu and cook just as you would scrambled eggs. Purée again. Drain potatoes and mash or purée. Mix with tofu. Dry the mixture by stirring for a few minutes in a pan over low heat. When most of the moisture is eliminated, stir in butter, salt and pepper. Beat yogurt until smooth, then stir into the tofu/potato purée. Add chopped herbs.

Tofu Sandwich

Slice tofu into sandwich sized portions, fry in olive oil or butter, garnish with favorite seasonings (such as salt, lemon pepper, or Italian Herbal Dressing, page 210). Add your usual favorite sandwich toppings such as lettuce, tomatoes and black olives, and other favorite condiments.

Tofu "Chicken" Pasta Salad with Curry Dressing

3 ounces rotelle pasta
1 tablespoon vegetable oil
1 ½ teaspoons curry powder
⅜ cup mayonnaise
1 ¼ teaspoons salt
1 teaspoon tarragon leaves, crushed
¼ teaspoon ground black pepper
1 pound fresh tofu, well drained and cubed
1 ½ cups cooked broccoli florets
¾ cup red bell pepper
chicken bouillon cube or chicken spices, optional

Cook and drain pasta according to package directions, then place in a large bowl. In small skillet heat oil until hot. Add curry powder, cook and stir until spice is fragrant, about 30 seconds. Transfer to small bowl and add mayonnaise and spices. Add tofu, broccoli and peppers to pasta. Stir in seasoned mayonnaise.

Hot "Chicken" Pasta Salad

If you prefer to serve the recipe as a hot dish, follow directions above but also sauté the tofu in the oil and seasonings and mix all ingredients together.

"Chicken" Roll-Ups

This recipe has a lot of potential for variation. Mix or match your favorite ingredients. If you don't have time to make crêpes, then use tortillas.

1 pound (fresh or frozen) tofu, drained and cubed in small pieces
1 tablespoons freshly squeezed lime juice
1 teaspoon grated lime peel
salt and pepper to taste
¼ teaspoon paprika
1 medium-size avocado
1 medium size red bell pepper, diced (about ¾ cup)
½ cup fresh or frozen corn kernels, thawed
1 tablespoon chopped fresh cilantro or parsley
crêpes (see recipe below) or packaged wheat tortillas
4 tablespoons prepared chili sauce or salsa
½ cup sour cream

Marinate tofu at least 15 minutes in lime juice, grated lime peel, salt and paprika. Mix avocado, pepper, corn, 2 tablespoons lime juice, cilantro and remaining salt. Set aside. Drain tofu and broil for 2 to 4 minutes, basting it with marinade if necessary to keep it moist. Place crêpes or tortillas flat on work surface, brush each with 1 tablespoon chili sauce or salsa. Wrap tofu in the crêpes or tortillas. Place, seam side down, in a 13 x 9 baking dish. Spoon 2 tablespoons sour cream over each roll-up, topping with about ¼ cup salsa. Bake, covered at 350° for 10 to 15 minutes until heated through.

Crêpes

Combine ¼ cup milk, 2 large eggs or egg substitute,⅓ cup flour, ¼ teaspoon salt, ⅛ teaspoon paprika, and 1 tablespoon melted butter in blender. Blend until smooth. Set 9-inch crêpe pan or skillet over medium heat, brush lightly with melted butter. Pour 2 to 3 tablespoons crêpe batter into heated skillet or crêpe pan. Over medium heat, cook about 30 seconds or until top of crêpe loses its shine and edge can be lifted easily with small spatula. Turn. Cook 20 to 20 seconds longer. Remove crêpe to plate, repeat with remaining crêpe batter.

Herbed Tofu-Chicken Strips

Tofu can be used in any recipe calling for poultry.

1 ¼ cup oats, uncooked
1 ¼ teaspoons basil
1 teaspoons paprika
½ teaspoons oregano
½ teaspoons thyme
½ pound fresh or frozen tofu, drained, and cut into ¾ inch strips
¼ cup milk
¼ cup margarine, melted
salt and pepper to taste

Place oats in blender or food processor bowl, cover, and blend about 1 minute, stopping occasionally to stir. Mix spices into oat mixture. Dip tofu into oat mixture, then into milk, then again into the oat mixture. Place in shallow baking pan, drizzle with margarine or butter. Bake at 425° for 25 or 30 minutes, or until crispy.

Optional Tomato Sauce for Herbed Tofu Chicken Strips

1 8-ounce can tomato sauce
½ finely chopped green pepper
½ teaspoons basil
salt and pepper to taste

Simmer for ten minutes and serve with tofu strips.

Tofu "Turkey" soup

½ to 1 pound diced tofu
2 medium potatoes, cut into chunks
2 medium carrots, sliced
2 stalks celery, sliced
1 green pepper, diced
1 zucchini, diced
1 teaspoon basil
½ teaspoon oregano
¼/ teaspoon paprika
salt and pepper to taste
butter, margarine, or ghee (clarified butter; recipe on page 216)

Boil potatoes, carrots, and half of celery and green pepper for ten minutes, then add remaining ingredients except spices and cook until tender. Sauté tofu in butter, margarine, or ghee, with spices, and add to soup. To make thicker soup, add 1 tablespoon flour.

Tofu Balls

1 cup milk
1 cup mashed potatoes
1 ½ teaspoon salt
½ teaspoon ground black pepper
1 egg or egg substitute
vegetable or olive oil

Heat oil in saucepan. Add cabbage, celery, and bean sprouts. Sauté 3 minutes. Add broth, soy sauce, and chili peppers. Cook over low heat 15 minutes. Chop the tofu. Soak the bread in milk or potato water and mash. Mix potatoes, tofu, salt, pepper, egg or egg substitute. Shape into 1 inch balls. Heat remaining oil in skillet. Brown the balls over medium to high heat.

Tofu and Pineapple

Tofu works well in almost any oriental dish. You can almost always use it even if the recipe doesn't specifically call for it.

1 pound tofu
3 tablespoons oil
1 (16-ounce) can diced pineapple
2 tablespoons lime or lemon juice
2 tablespoons lime or lemon rind, grated
2 cups coconut cream
2 teaspoons soy sauce

Sauté tofu and pineapple until slightly browned. Add juice, rind, cream, and soy sauce. Serve over rice.

Po Lo Ho

(Batter fried tofu with pineapple)

1 cup flour
1 teaspoon baking powder
1 ½ teaspoon salt (to be used in 2 portions)
1 egg or substitute, beaten
½ cup pineapple juice
1 ½ pound tofu
oil for deep frying
1 tablespoon cornstarch
1 tablespoon sugar
1 tablespoon lemon juice
½ cup pineapple juice
1 cup pineapple chunks

Stir flour, baking powder, and ½ teaspoon salt in a bowl. Beat in egg and pineapple juice. Dip tofu in the batter, coating it well. Heat the oil to 350° and fry the tofu until browned. Drain and keep warm.

Mix cornstarch, sugar and remaining salt with the lemon juice. Add pineapple juice and cook over low heat until thickened. Arrange the tofu and pineapple on a dish and pour sauce over all.

Tofu Balls in Vegetable Sauce

6 tablespoons oil
1 cup coarsely shredded cabbage
1 cup bean sprouts
1 cup diced celery
2 cups broth
1 tablespoon soy sauce
¼ teaspoon dried chilies
1 pound fresh tofu, drained
1 slice bread

¼ cup milk
1 cup mashed potatoes
1 ½ teaspoon salt
½ teaspoon ground black pepper
1 egg or egg substitute

Heat 3 tablespoons oil in saucepan. Add cabbage, celery, and bean sprouts. Sauté 3 minutes. Add broth, soy sauce, and chili peppers. Cook over low heat 15 minutes. Prepare tofu balls while veggies are cooking. Chop the tofu. Soak the bread in milk or potato water and mash. Mix with the potatoes, tofu, salt, pepper, and egg or egg substitute. Shape into 1-inch balls. Heat remaining oil in skillet and brown the balls. Add to the veggies. Cook over low heat for five minutes.

Tofu Curry

1 tablespoon ghee (clarified butter) or butter
1 teaspoon ground caraway seeds
1 teaspoon ground coriander
1 teaspoon lemon rind, grated
¼ teaspoon basil
¼ teaspoon black pepper
2 green bell peppers, chopped
¼ cup cabbage, finely shredded
5 cups coconut cream
1 pound tofu, drained and cubed

Sauté spices in ghee or butter. Add remaining ingredients and continue cooking until vegetables are tender.

Sharalyn Pliler

Curried Tofu and Avocado Salad

1 (9-ounce) can water chestnuts, drained and sliced
½ pound fresh or frozen tofu, drained and cubed
½ cup mayonnaise
1 tablespoon fresh lemon juice
¾ teaspoon curry powder
1 ½ teaspoon soy sauce
1 avocado, sliced
Lemon pepper to taste

Mix first 6 ingredients. Serve mixture on lettuce leaf with slices of tomato, with avocado on top. Lightly sprinkle with lemon pepper.

Care of Tofu

Tofu is fully cooked when you purchase it. After opening, to prevent spoilage it must be kept in water and the water changed if not daily at least every couple of days. Tofu keeps for up to two weeks with daily changes of water.

CHAPTER 8
How To Make Meat and Egg Substitutes from Tofu

"Tastes like meat to me!"

After becoming a vegetarian, I felt lighter and healthier and I knew I'd made the right decision, but I still missed favorite meat foods like tacos, pizza, and chili. A turning point toward more culinary satisfaction occurred when one day, my friend, Ed Hipp (then the kitchen director at Maharishi University of Management where I worked as a cook), put together something he called, with a wry grin, "Un-chicken Soup." Made from vegetables, spices, soy sauce and bits of tofu, his soup tasted so much like chicken soup the staff gathered around the pot and it was gone in minutes. Like Oliver in Dickens's story, Great Expectations, we held out our bowls and begged, "More!"

But there was no more, and what was worse was that no more could be made. It had been one of those "a bit of this and a pinch of that" accidents of fate, a masterpiece of culinary pleasure that no one have been able to recreate since. But even though the recipe for the great Un-chicken Soup may be lost for all time, it had the effect of showing me that with the right combinations of herbs, spices, and other good ingredients, *tofu could be made to taste like meat.* I began my own experimentation, and the following original recipes are the result. You may find this to be one of the most useful chapters in this book (and there are some really good chapters in it) so try these recipes. If you don't want to take the time to create my meat substitute, then you can use TVP (Textured Vegetable Protein), a soy-based meat substitute in the freezer or dry bulk section of the grocery store or at your local health food store.

Making meat substitutes with tofu

Freezing and then thawing tofu gives it a fibrous texture that looks like bread and chews like meat. By capitalizing on this meat-like texture you can create a ground beef substitute with a hearty, meaty flavor that will work in all your favorite ground beef recipes. Tofu ground beef is so good that when it was used in my chili recipe, five out of six taste testers didn't know it wasn't meat.

Tofu Ground Beef

1 pound tofu
vegetable oil
1 ½ teaspoons rubbed sage or 1 teaspoon ground sage
1 teaspoon thyme
½ teaspoon celery seed
2 tablespoons soy sauce or vegetable protein sauce

Freeze the tofu in its package at least 48 hours before use, and then thaw. Drain, then press or wring out remaining water until the tofu is dry. After removing excess water, shred it with a food processor or a hand-held grater until it has the consistency of crumbled ground beef.

Heat oil enough to prevent sticking, and add tofu. Cook until the tofu is a light golden brown, stirring frequently. Sprinkle herbs, then drizzle soy sauce over the tofu bits and mix well.

Taste Testing

Are you surprised that the result looks like ground beef? Now, throw away your expectations so your first bite is a new experience. What you may experience is, "Aha! This is delicious—what meaty texture and flavor! Why, I bet this would work great in chili, or ground beef casseroles or tacos or … " Then experiment—use it in all your favorite recipes that call for ground beef or sausage.

Ground Beef Stuffed Peppers

Remember my story about how much I once disliked bell peppers? This recipe with bell peppers is now one of my all-time favorite recipes.

1 pound tofu ground beef
4 large or 6 small bell peppers
2 cups cooked rice
1 shredded carrot
1 stalk celery, finely chopped
1 teaspoon marjoram
2 (8-ounce) cans tomato sauce
¼ teaspoon pepper
Small amount of vegetable oil

Sauté carrots and celery in vegetable oil, add marjoram, tofu ground beef, rice, and one can tomato sauce, and mix well. Remove tops from the green peppers, or cut peppers in two lengthwise, and remove seeds. Stuff pepper shells with tofu mixture. Pour remaining tomato sauce over the tops as a sealer. Bake in 350° oven for one hour or until peppers are tender.

Corn Stuffed Tofu Peppers

Follow recipe above except add 1 cup fresh or frozen corn. Important: warm the corn before mixing it into the stuffing.

Tofu Sloppy Joes

The combination of cooked and raw peppers in this dish adds both flavor and a fresh tang. You can use this idea of adding some raw foods in other dishes too.

1 pound tofu hamburger
2-8 ounce cans tomato sauce
½ to 1 green pepper chopped, divided in 2 portions

Cook tofu hamburger as directed on page 72, adding ½ the pepper and cooking until tender. When done, add the tomato sauce, warm. Add remaining peppers before serving. Spread over bread and eat with a fork.

Pizza

Ah, Pizza. Who would ever want to be a vegetarian if they had to give up pizza? Fortunately, we can set our taste buds to "great new flavors" and continue to enjoy pizza that is not only tasty but also healthy. Furthermore, with a little experimentation, you can learn to make pizza from scratch—crust, sauce, and all—to meet your own exacting taste standards. Start with this recipe, then add or change toppings until you find which ones you like best.

Easy Pizza

Cover homemade, packaged, or frozen crust with one cup (more or less) of your favorite pizza or spaghetti sauce. Then sprinkle liberally with:

- mozzarella cheese, shredded
- black olives, sliced
- green peppers, diced
- tofu ground beef or sausage (page 83)
- chunk pineapple, well drained
- eggplant (optional), diced small
- zucchini (optional), thin sliced

Sprinkle completed pizza with 2 tablespoons olive oil and bake at 425° for 15 minutes, or until crust is brown and veggies are done.

Tofu Stuffed Italian Meat Loaf

If you don't tell your guests this recipe is not made from beef, they actually may not know the difference.

1 pound tofu ground beef
1 cup oatmeal
1 (15-ounce) can tomato sauce
½ cup sliced ripe olives
½ cup mozzarella cheese, shredded
½ cup shredded zucchini (optional); pressed dry
⅓ cup Parmesan cheese
1 egg (or substitute)
1 tablespoon Worcestershire sauce (optional)
1 teaspoon black pepper

Heat oven to 350°. Reserve ⅓ of the tomato sauce and a little of the cheese and olives for toppings. Combine remaining ingredients. Grease loaf pan and fill with mixture, covering it with remaining sauce and garnishes. Bake 45 minutes to one hour, or until well browned and firm.

(Note: Mix ingredients only when you are ready to bake, otherwise it will come out soggy.)

Gourmet Tofu Stuffed Italian Meat Loaf

Mix ingredients in recipe above, reserving the olives, mozzarella, and zucchini. Divide the tofu into two portions, pressing one half into the loaf pan. Form a concave area in it (like a nest) in which to place the olives, mozzarella and zucchini. Cover with the second patty, then spread remaining sauce and toppings over the whole. Bake as directed.

Tofu Ground Beef Chili

"I really thought it was hamburger," guests say with surprise when, after the meal, I inform them this recipe is made with tofu. (Note: I always alert my vegetarian friends ahead of time that it is tofu, not hamburger.)

1 pound prepared tofu ground beef
2 cups pinto beans, uncooked
1 (6-ounce) can tomato paste
1 (16-ounce) can tomatoes, cut up
1 teaspoon cumin
¼ teaspoon black pepper
1 green pepper, diced
prepared or homemade (page 227) chili mix, to taste

Cook beans following directions on package. In the last half hour of cooking, add remaining ingredients except tofu. Just before serving add 1 pound of tofu ground beef.

Serve with cornbread or crackers.

Tofu Lasagna

I bet you'll be surprised at how gourmet this is.

3 cups Ricotta or cottage cheese
6 lasagna noodles
1 jar prepared or 4 cups homemade spaghetti sauce
1 pound tofu ground beef
2 cups shredded mozzarella
½ cup Parmesan or Romano cheese

Cook lasagna according to package instructions. Mix tofu ground beef into spaghetti sauce. Mix together Ricotta or cottage cheese and mozzarella. In oiled 13 x 9 baking dish layer noodles, sauce, and cheese mixture. Sprinkle all with grated Parmesan or Romano cheese. Bake at 375° for 30 to 40 minutes, or until the cottage cheese melts.

Optional layer: use an 8-ounce tub of sour cream, or a 16-ounce for a thicker layer.

Tofu Ground Beef Spaghetti

Mix 1 pound tofu ground beef into 1 ½ cups spaghetti sauce. Serve over 12 ounces of cooked spaghetti.

Serving suggestion: Serve Tofu Lasagna or Spaghetti with Parmesan cheese on the side, salad, and Italian Bread.

Tofu Tacos

Add prepared or home-made taco seasoning (see page 227) to taste, to one pound prepared tofu ground beef. Add 4 tablespoons salsa. Serve warm with side dishes of:

lettuce, finely chopped
green peppers, diced small
black olives, chopped
fresh tomatoes, diced
cheddar cheese, shredded
sour cream
warmed taco shells

Tofu Hamburger Taco Casserole

This is another dish that is simple enough for everyday but good enough for guests … and I've yet to have anyone ask, "But where's the beef?"

1 pound tofu ground beef
1 cup pinto, red, or kidney beans, uncooked
1 cup corn, frozen or fresh
½ (16-ounce) can black olives
1 green pepper, diced
1 (16-ounce) can or 3 fresh tomatoes, diced
¾ cup cheddar cheese, shredded
prepared taco spice to taste
black pepper to taste
taco shells, broken

Cook beans until tender. Sauté green peppers, zucchini, corn, and spices in vegetable oil. Purée 1 cup cooked beans, adding liquid if necessary. Mix purée with remainder of beans, adding the tofu ground beef, tomatoes, olives and vegetable/spice mixture. In oiled deep casserole dish layer bean mixture, broken taco shells, and cheese, ending with a layer of cheese. Bake at 350° for 1 hour. Add broken taco shells before baking or serve them on the side. Sliced avocados are nice additions too.

Optional: add a tub of sour cream as one of the layers.

Tofu "Beefsteak"

Tofu beefsteak, served with mashed potatoes and beef gravy, has a hearty, meaty texture that former meat eaters find really satisfying.

- 1 pound tofu, frozen and thawed
- ¼ cup soy sauce or vegetable protein sauce
- ¼ cup water
- ¾ teaspoon black pepper
- 2 teaspoons cumin
- 2 teaspoons coriander
- 1 cup flour
- 2 tablespoons vegetable oil

Slice tofu into ¼- to ½-inch slices. Wring or press each slice until it is dry. Mix soy sauce and water and add herbs and spices. Roll tofu in soy sauce mixture, then in flour. Fry in oil over medium heat until browned.

Smothered Tofu Beefsteak

Cover Tofu Beefsteak with gravy. Even your most macho guest may not realize this gravy isn't made from beef.

"Beef" Gravy

4 tablespoons oil
½ teaspoon black pepper
1 teaspoon cumin
1 teaspoon coriander
3 tablespoons flour
¼ cup soy sauce
3 cups water

Add flour and spices to oil heated over medium heat. Stir until slightly browned. Add soy sauce and water and continue cooking until thickened.

Spoon gravy liberally over Tofu Beefsteak and mashed potatoes.

> ***Menu Suggestion: For a good old-fashioned "meat and potatoes"-style dinner, serve Tofu Beefsteak with mashed potatoes, peas, salad, and apple pie.***

Tofu Pepper Steak

There are endless ways to use tofu as a meat substitute. This is another one of my favorite recipes.

1 pound tofu (frozen, thawed, wrung or pressed dry then cubed)
2 large green peppers, cut into large chunks
1 medium zucchini, sliced (optional)

Cut tofu into bite-sized pieces and follow directions above for making tofu beefsteak. Add peppers and zucchini and cook until crisp-tender. Use the recipe for beef gravy above to create a sauce for the pepper steak, add steak and vegetables, and mix well.

Spoon mixture over a bed of hot rice.

Tofu Fried Chicken Morsels

Preparing tofu this way gives it a delicious "chickeny" taste with a satisfying crunch.

1 pound tofu (frozen, thawed, wrung or pressed dry)
1 cup flour
1 cup water
1 teaspoon oregano
½ teaspoon rosemary
½ teaspoon salt
½ teaspoon thyme
¼ teaspoon sage
¼ teaspoon pepper

Mix flour, water and herbs into smooth paste. Cut tofu into small cubes and coat with flour mixture. Cook in skillet in butter or margarine until golden brown. Serve as a fried chicken substitute or in recipes such as Chicken Pot Pie.

Another Style Tofu Chicken

It is the flour mixture that gives tofu chicken its crunch, but anytime you need to replace the chicken in a favorite recipe, try this: using the same spices listed above, sauté the herbs and spices in butter or margarine. Cube fresh or frozen (and thawed) tofu, and add to spices. Continue to cook for about 5 to 10 minutes until tofu has absorbed herb flavors. Use in any recipe that calls for chicken.

Tofu Chicken Pot Pie

Steaming hot out of the oven, this dish will make warm, loving memories.

- 2 potatoes, diced
- 2 carrots, diced
- 2 celery, sliced
- ½ green pepper, diced
- ½ pound prepared tofu chicken (from "chicken recipe)
- 4 tablespoons butter

Simmer vegetables until tender, then combine with tofu in 13 x 9 baking dish, including water. Cover with homemade or canned biscuits and bake at 450° for 10 to 15 minutes, or until biscuits are golden brown. For a thicker "soup," mix 1 or 2 tablespoons flour in ¼ cup water and add to the water covering the vegetables.

Tofu Shrimp Gumbo

- 2 teaspoons French's "Crab Boil" seasoning mixture (or any Creole spice mix to taste)
- 1 (16-ounce) can tomatoes
- ½ pound tofu, fresh or frozen and thawed
- 1 medium zucchini, sliced
- 8 okra, sliced
- 1 stalk celery, sliced
- ½ teaspoon salt
- ½ teaspoon sugar

In blender, purée "Crab Boil" seasoning mixture (or substitute any Creole spice mix, to taste) and blend with tomatoes until smooth. Add blender contents to other ingredients in large saucepan and simmer until vegetables are done and tofu has absorbed flavors.

Serve as is, or over rice.

Tofu Sausage

Try this on sandwiches or in recipes calling for ground beef.

1 pound frozen tofu, thawed, wrung dry, and crumbled
1 ½ teaspoons ginger
1 ½ teaspoons black pepper
½ teaspoon sage
½ teaspoon rosemary
½ teaspoon thyme
½ teaspoon tarragon
½ teaspoon dry mustard
2 tablespoon soy or vegetable protein sauce
oil sufficient to keep tofu from sticking

Freeze the tofu in its package at least 48 hours before use. Thaw, drain, then press or wring out the remaining water until the tofu is very dry. After pressing, shred it with a food processor or a hand-held grater until it has the consistency of crumbled ground beef.

Heat oil enough to prevent sticking and add tofu. Cook until the tofu is a light golden brown, stirring frequently. Sprinkle herbs, then drizzle soy sauce over the tofu pieces and mix well.

Tofu Goulash

2 cups noodles
1 (8-ounce) can tomato sauce
½ pound prepared tofu sausage or ground beef

Cook noodles following instructions on the package. When tender, add remaining ingredients and mix well. Heat again if necessary.

Tofu Quiche

If you like egg quiche, you'll like tofu quiche.

1 pound fresh, soft tofu
1 cup Swiss cheese, shredded
1 cup broccoli, cut into small florets
1 cup cauliflower, cut into small florets
½ green pepper, diced
2 stalks celery, sliced
1 box frozen spinach, thawed and drained, or 4 cups fresh spinach
1 teaspoon oil
1 teaspoon cornstarch
¼ teaspoon celery seed
½ teaspoon nutmeg
½ teaspoon ground mustard
¼ teaspoon pepper

Drain spinach well and set aside. (If using fresh spinach, steam just until limp.) Purée tofu with oil and spices until smooth and stir in remaining ingredients. Spread into oiled pie pan and bake 45 minutes to an hour at 375°. For egg-like color, add ¼ teaspoon turmeric.

This recipe can also be made without the broccoli and/or cauliflower.

Scrambled Egg-fu

To create "scrambled" eggs, use fresh tofu. To get an "eggier" taste, use margarine rather than butter.

1 pound fresh tofu, drained
½ teaspoon thyme
¼ teaspoon celery seed
⅛ teaspoon turmeric
⅓ cup milk
salt and pepper to taste
margarine to coat skillet

Heat margarine in skillet. Crumble tofu in small pieces into skillet. Add ingredients and cook/stir until it has the consistency of scrambled eggs.

Fancy Scrambled Egg-fu

If you want to get fancy, add veggies like celery, green peppers, squash, or whatever suits your taste.

I highly recommend that you use fresh ingredients, but if you are accustomed to using packaged foods, here are other meat substitute ideas:

- Add tofu ground beef to Hamburger Helper.
- Use fresh tofu instead of tuna in Tuna Helper.
- Use fresh or "chicken" flavored tofu in Chicken Tonight simmer sauces.

You can also:

- Use tofu ground beef in any of your favorite ground beef recipes.

- Use tofu "chicken" in any favorite chicken recipes.
- Use tofu "steak" in any favorite beef recipes.
- For quicker fixes, use beef- or chicken-flavored TVP products (from your health food store or from the freezer or produce section in the grocery store) in place of tofu "meat" recipes.

CHAPTER 9
Sources of Protein: Beans & Peas

"Read this chapter if you know what's good for you".

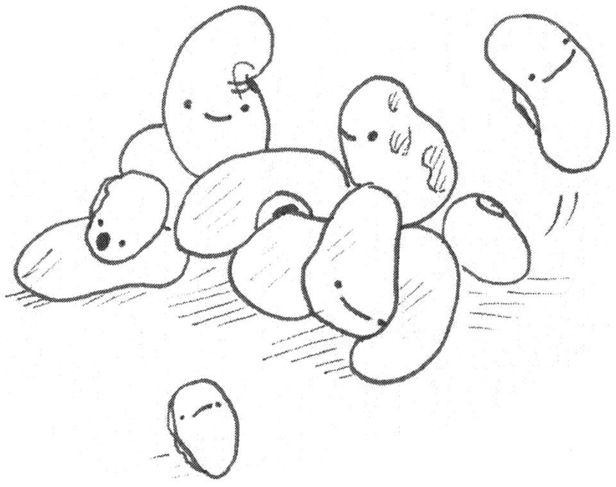

In the food group pyramid on the poster in high school health class, I thought the beans looked very small and unimportant compared to the meat, cheese, milk and eggs. I knew beans were great for a barbeque or a down-home dinner, served with fried 'taters and cornbread, or baked with mustard and molasses. But I essentially thought of them as a "poor man's" food ... and as a poor substitute for meat.

But since then I have discovered that beans are far too versatile, interesting and nutritive to be limited to just traditional favorite side dishes. Far from being a mere substitute for meat, beans are excellent sources of nutrition, and it's fun watching faces light up with surprise when guests try my *Lima Bean Casserole* or enjoy the hearty richness of *Black Bean Soup*.

Advantages of beans:

- Beans are rich in protein. The average protein content in most beans is 22 percent by weight, up to 40 percent for soybeans.
- Beans are easy to prepare. Wash, boil until tender, and eat. Even easier, they can be left in a slow cooker (on low) to cook untended overnight or while you are at work.
- Beans are economical, costing less than any other protein source.
- The skin of beans contains antioxidants that protect cells from damage caused by free radicals.

Learning to use beans in a wide variety of ways means good taste, good nutrition, and good time- and money-management.

Cooking Beans and Peas

Beans should be sorted and washed before cooking. Watch for, and remove, any small pieces of gravel.

Soaking insures that beans will cook evenly. The bean can absorb water and become tender only through the point at which it was attached to its pod. Soak all beans except lentils, split beans, and peas, in cold water for 8 to 12 hours before cooking.

A faster soaking method is to boil the beans for two to ten minutes, cover, then set aside for an hour. Whichever method you use, after soaking, drain and replace the water before further cooking.

(Note: Soaking beans with ¼ teaspoon of soda mixed in the water reportedly helps to prevent flatulence.)

Other useful information about beans:

- Soak beans in at least 3 times as much water as the volume of beans. Dried beans swell approximately two and one half times.
- 1 pound of beans makes 4 to 6 cups cooked beans.
- Add a bit of vegetable oil or butter while cooking to prevent foaming.
- Avoid cooking at too high heat as this can break the skins.
- Old beans take longer to cook than new beans, so don't mix old and new.
- Beans don't cook well in a microwave.
- Add a few beans to any soup to add body and flavor.

Safety Tip For Beans

Legumes contain lectins, a toxin which can cause stomach cramps and other discomforts. Fortunately, lectins are destroyed at high temperatures, so boiling them for a few minutes is enough to prevent problems. After boiling, beans can be simmered, slow-cooked, baked, or boiled until tender. Small beans such as lentils and peas require only a brief boil, larger beans need ten minutes.

Now, throw away all your concepts about beans and see if after trying these recipes you don't have a new appreciation for this great food.

Bean Chart

Name	Unique Features	Cook Time
Black Beans	Tender, almost sweet; use in thick soups, rice, cheese, Oriental, Mediterranean, dishes.	1 ½ hours
Great Northern	Soups, casseroles	1 ½-2 hours
Kidney	Meaty texture, sweet taste; Good baked or in salads	1 ½-2 hours
Lima	Good as main dish, casseroles	1 hour
Mung	Fresh flavor	½ hour
Navy	Smooth tasting, versatile	1 ½-2 hours
Pinto	Good plain, spiced, or in chili	1 ½-2 hrs
Red Beans	Good plain, spiced, in salads	1 ½-2 hours
Lentils, split	Excellent source of protein, iron, potassium, no soaking required Great in soups.	20-25 min.
Lentils, whole	Meaty flavor, use as substitute for potatoes, rice, meat.	30 min. 35 for purée
Black-eyed Peas	Too strong for some folks	1 ½-2 hours
Split Peas	Great for soups or dahls. No soaking required; stir to prevent burning.	Simmer, 30-40 min., 45 for purée
Dahls	Several varieties, no soaking required, good curries	simmer 40 min. – 1 hr.

A final note on beans: adding a pinch of sugar has a nice effect.

Lentil Tacos

Lentils have a surprisingly meaty flavor and work very well with Mexican spices. Try them in this recipe then use them as substitutes for meat in all your favorite Mexican dishes.

1 cup lentils, uncooked
1 teaspoon oregano
1 teaspoon chili powder or 1 tablespoon store-bought or homemade (page 227) taco spices
salt and pepper to taste

(Note; you'll need less or no extra pepper at all if you use homemade taco spices.)

Cook lentils. When tender, drain and purée into a paste, or use whole. Stir in spices. Serve hot in a bowl surrounded by the fixings and lots of napkins. Serve on warmed taco shells with diced tomatoes, minced green pepper, shredded lettuce or sprouts, minced black olives and sour cream.

Bean Pancakes (Re-fried beans)

Bring cooked pinto beans (salted and spiced as desired) to a boil in a greased skillet, mash with pestle or potato masher into a course purée. Serve as is or continue cooking under lower heat until the beans dry and form a thick pancake. Serve with salsa.

Sharalyn Pliler

Mexican Roll-ups

This is a fun, pretty dish that can be made with any combination of Mexican ingredients.

1 16-ounce package or 3 cups dry lentils
3 tablespoons homemade chili powder or packaged taco spices to taste
1 teaspoon oregano
1 teaspoon cumin
1 teaspoon salt
¼ teaspoon pepper
½ cup frozen corn
1 green pepper, chopped
1 fresh tomato, chopped
6 flour tortillas or soft taco shells
1 16-ounce jar salsa
1 16-ounce tub sour cream

optional: cheddar cheese
black olives
chopped avocado

Cook lentils and spices until tender and beans are thick, then mix in remaining ingredients. Spoon mixture into shells, then wrap the shells around it. Lay into a 13 x 9 pan and cover with salsa and sour cream. Bake at 375° for 30 minutes.

Navy Bean Soup

1 pound navy beans
½ cup cooked and mashed potatoes
3 cups chopped celery
¼ cup chopped fresh parsley
2 teaspoons salt
dash pepper

After beans are cooked, add remaining ingredients and mix well. You may continue cooking until celery is done, or leave it raw to add a lively, fresh flavor.

Optional: add sliced or diced carrots, bok choy, green peppers, and finely chopped greens. Almost any vegetable can be used to create unique flavors and increase nutrition.

A Different Three-Bean Salad, with Lemon Dressing

2 cups cooked lentils, drained
1 cup cooked black beans, drained
1 cup chick peas, drained
¾ cup roasted green pepper strips

Dressing: Mix ¼ cup olive oil, ½ teaspoon grated lemon peel, 3 tablespoons lemon juice and ⅛ teaspoon pepper.

Mix beans and peppers in a 2-quart casserole. Combine oil, lemon with grated peel, and black pepper, and add to bean mixture. Toss together well.

Pepper Pot Soup, an Easy Favorite

1 ½ cups uncooked lentils
1 large potato, diced
2 small or 1 large carrot, sliced
1 stalk celery
1 pepper, diced
1 (16-ounce) can tomatoes, quartered
½ teaspoon savory
¼ teaspoon thyme
1 bay leaf
1 tablespoon butter
salt and pepper to taste

Boil lentils, then simmer until tender. Add vegetables (including the liquid from the tomatoes), butter, and spices.

Optional: For a thicker soup add ¾ cup uncooked barley at beginning of cooking.

Black Bean Soup

This is such a rich and hearty soup it always makes me glad I became a vegetarian. To make it smoother and thicker, purée ¼ of the cooked beans.

1 ½ cups uncooked black turtle beans
2 carrots, sliced
1 green pepper, diced
1 teaspoon cumin
½ teaspoon marjoram
½ teaspoon thyme
1 tablespoon fresh or ½ teaspoon dried parsley
1 (6-ounce) can tomato paste
1 teaspoon cooking oil
1 teaspoon salt
¼ teaspoon pepper

For an unforgettable soup, add one cup barley 40 minutes before beans are done.

Optional: 1 teaspoon cinnamon (your first reaction may be that cinnamon and beans don't mix, but try this—it's delicious.)

Lima Bean Casserole

How surprised I was to find that beans could taste like this. It sure is different than the hillbilly beans and cornbread meals I knew as a child.

1 pound lima beans
2 cups cooked rice
1 16-ounce tub sour cream
¾ cup white cheese (mozzarella, Muenster, or jack, or other favorite), shredded
1 tablespoon caraway seeds
2 tablespoons butter
1 teaspoon salt
¼ teaspoon pepper
water, enough to make a thick gravy

Cook beans and rice. Melt butter and add sour cream and water (mixed to gravy consistency). Mix into cooked beans and grain.

Fast-Track Mexican Salad

This is a fun, quick recipe for picnics, covered dish dinners, and company whose arrival time is indefinite. To prevent sogginess, prepare ingredients ahead of time but wait to mix them until just before you need them so all the ingredients are fresh and crisp.

½ head lettuce, cut up for salad
1 tomato, diced
2 to 3 cups kidney or red beans, cooked and drained
1 bell pepper, diced
1 cup cheddar or other cheese, cubed
French dressing or salsa to taste
corn chips

Mix ingredients and serve.

This is a salad that invites personal creativity. Add any favorite ingredient. For instance, you could dress it up with artichoke hearts, cucumbers, cherry tomatoes, or any other salad food that appeals to you.

Mexican Casserole

This is a great casserole for family or guests. It's full of healthy ingredients, can be made in a hurry, and is always delicious.

1 pound brown or kidney beans, cooked
½ medium zucchini, sliced
½ cup frozen corn
1 green pepper, chopped
1 (16-ounce) can tomatoes or one large fresh tomato, chopped
¾ cup cheddar cheese, shredded
1 cup black olives
2 tablespoons homemade chili powder/taco mix (page 227) or store-bought, to taste
1 teaspoon cumin
1 teaspoon oregano
1 teaspoon salt
¼ teaspoon pepper
corn tortillas or chips, crisp

Cook beans with spices until tender and the liquid is thick. Add remaining ingredients except cheese and tortillas. Pour into a casserole dish, sprinkle with cheese, and bake at 375° for 1 hour.

Bean Tostados

This is such a delicious recipe, and so easy.

1 pound bag brown or kidney beans
1 green pepper, chopped

1 large fresh tomato, chopped
1 cup black olives
2 tablespoons homemade chili/taco powder (page 227) store-bought taco spices, to taste
1 teaspoon cumin
1 teaspoon oregano
¼ teaspoon pepper
1 cup cheddar cheese, shredded
tortilla chips

Boil then simmer beans until tender. Drain and save liquid. Purée beans, adding liquid as needed. Sauté green pepper, tomatoes and spices in oil, then mix into bean mixture. Add olives. In oiled 13 x 9 pan layer the sour cream, tortilla chips, beans, and cheese, ending with cheese. Bake at 350° for 1 hour or until cheese is melted.

Cornbread Lentil Pie

Isn't it wonderful to have recipes that are both quick *and* tasty?

1 package lentils, cooked
1 (6-ounce) can tomato paste
1 green pepper, diced
3 tablespoons homemade chili/taco powder (page 227) or store-bought taco spices to taste
1 teaspoon oregano
1 teaspoon cumin
1 teaspoon salt
¼ teaspoon pepper

Sauté green peppers and spices, add to cooked beans and tomato paste. Pour mixture into a 9 x13 baking dish. Drizzle cornbread batter evenly over the bean mixture. Bake at 425° for 20 minutes or until cornbread has risen to the top and browned.

Cheese-Bean Patties

With this recipe, who needs cheeseburgers?

1 cup grated cheese, any kind
1 ½ cup cooked beans, any kind
1 ½ cup mashed potatoes
½ cup chopped green peppers
salt and pepper to taste

Mix ingredients together, roll in flour or cornmeal, and fry in oil until brown

Dahl

Dahl may sound boring to conventional Western tastes, but for nearly 6,000 years it has been daily fare for millions of East Indians. The reason it has stood the test of time is because, eaten with rice, it is easy to digest, especially satisfying, and "karma free." This means that it won't throw your body out of balance.

Rice and dahl is an easy, basic meal that can have an infinite number of variations in spices, added vegetables, and toppings such as shredded coconut, avocados, and churnas (spice mixtures, which you can make yourself [page 225] or purchase already prepared.)

Mung Dahl

Any bean can be used to make dahl but Mung Dahl (using split mung beans) is my favorite. For variety, add any veggie or spice mixture.

1 cup dry split mung beans, washed
4 cups water

1 ½ teaspoon salt, or to taste
2 teaspoon mild curry power or 1 teaspoon hot curry powder
1 teaspoon ginger
1 teaspoon cumin
1 teaspoon black mustard seeds (optional)
1 teaspoon ghee (page 216)

Cook dahl beans until tender, then purée, or if you are lazy, forget the puréeing—just cook until the beans have become mushy. Stir often when they begin to be mushy. One foolproof method it is to bring it to a boil then turn off the heat. Cover tightly and let sit for approximately 2 hours.

Italian Bean Soup

Dressier than plain beans but still goood with cornbread and coleslaw.

1 pound dry lima beans
2 medium carrots, sliced
2 stalks celery, sliced
2 tomatoes, chopped
1 teaspoon basil
½ teaspoon savory
1 tablespoon olive oil

Boil then simmer beans. When beans nearly tender, add vegetables and spices and simmer until veggies are tender.

Black Eyed Peas, Cabbage, and Cheese

In Iowa, where I live, the custom is to eat black-eyed peas on New Year's Day. This is my favorite black-eyed pea recipe.

1 pound black-eyed peas
½ large head cabbage, chopped
1 cup cheese, shredded
1 tablespoon caraway seed
salt and pepper to taste

Boil beans, then simmer until tender. Drain off excess liquid, leaving enough to barely cover beans. Mix in cabbage, cheese, and spices. Pour mixture into a 13 x 9 casserole dish and bake 350° for 1 hour or until cheese has melted.

Lentil Burgers

Burgers can be made from any bean, any vegetable, any cheese, even nuts. You can go for any flavor—meaty, pungent, spicy hot, cheesy, and so forth. Just experiment until you find what flavors you like best.

½ pound lentils
2 stalks celery, minced
1 carrot, shredded
1 (6-ounce) can tomato paste
1 egg (or egg substitute plus one tablespoon flour)
¼ teaspoon savory
¼ teaspoon thyme
¼ teaspoon marjoram
salt to taste
¼ teaspoon pepper
1 cup cottage cheese

Simmer beans until tender, drain and mash or purée, adding liquid as needed. Sauté celery, carrots, and spices, and mix with lentils, flour, tomato paste, and cottage cheese. Form into patties (adding more flour if needed to hold them together) and cook over medium heat until brown.

Split Pea Fritters

2 cups dried green or yellow split peas
4 tablespoon butter
½ cup dry bread crumbs
1 tablespoon finely cut mix of fresh dill and parsley
2 eggs or egg substitutes, slightly beaten

Drain cooked beans and purée. Add butter, spices, 1 egg or substitute, and ½ of the bread crumbs. Shape batter into patties or fritters, dip into the remaining egg, then into remaining bread crumbs. Fry in butter to a golden brown.

Falafel (garbanzo "meat" balls)

Food is always best prepared fresh in your own kitchen. However, if you don't want to go to all the trouble of making falafels from scratch, there are some good pre-mixes found in health food stores and also now in many supermarkets.

2 cups garbanzo beans, soaked
½ cup cold water
2 tablespoons parsley
¼ teaspoon cumin
1 teaspoon salt
1 cup bread crumbs, dry
pita bread, sliced open at top
Tahini sauce, store-bought or homemade (page 216)

Soak beans overnight, then drain and grind in food chopper or blend in blender with ½ cup cold water until very fine. Add spices. Dip by teaspoonfuls into the breadcrumbs, rolling and shaping with fingers into 1-inch balls. Place on ungreased baking pan, cover and bake at 350° for 15 minutes. Turn and continue baking, uncovered, for ten minutes.

Fill Pita bread with 3 garbanzo "meat balls," diced cucumber, tomato, and lettuce, followed by 2 tablespoons of tahini sauce. Tahini is made from sesame butter; it may be either homemade or purchased.

CHAPTER 10
Sources of Protein: Cheese & Dairy

"Indeed, the power of cheese."

I love cheeses, don't you? They are easy to use, tasty and a good source of protein. For improved digestibility, choose softer cheeses; for weight control go for low-fat.

Rules of Tongue for cheese:

- *Cheese experts advise removing the cheese from the refrigerator at least an hour before serving in order for the full flavor to be released.*
- *The softer the cheese the less length of time it "keeps," so plan accordingly after purchasing.*

Milk

In Ayurveda, the world's oldest comprehensive health system, milk is highly prized as a pure and nurturing food. However, some people find that milk causes mucus, weight gain, or other problems, so consult your body to see if it's for you. If the aftereffects of eating dairy are not satisfying to you, use milk alternatives.

Rules of Tongue for Milk:

- *For best digestibility, milk should not be eaten with mixed tastes, but only with sweet foods.*
- *To make milk more digestible, boil it and add a pinch of ginger.*
- *Avoid cold milk. Ayurvedic experts say that many milk allergies are caused from drinking milk cold right out of the refrigerator.*

Four Seasons Casserole

Use whatever vegetables are in season or on hand for this cassarole. Seems like no matter what veggies you use, this recipe comes out tasting great.

1 ½ cup eggplant or broccoli or cauliflower, cubed
or cut into florets.
1 medium zucchini, sliced

2 (8-ounce) cans tomatoes, drained and quartered
1 cup cooked grain (rice or barley)
2 cups cottage cheese
¼ teaspoon celery seed
½ teaspoon marjoram

Mix ingredients. Place in a lightly oiled 13 x 9 baking pan. Sprinkle with bread crumbs if desired. Bake at 350° for 45 to 60 minutes, or until cheese has melted.

Stuffed Cabbage

Nearly everyone who tries this asks for the recipe, even a few who claim to dislike cabbage. The ingredients really complement each other, or as great chefs say, they "marry well."

1 medium head cabbage
2 cups cooked rice
2 ½ cups shredded mozzarella or Muenster cheese (These cheeses are also good mixed half and half.)
2 tablespoons caraway seed
salt and pepper to taste
2-3 tablespoons butter, margarine or ghee
1 (15-ounce) can tomato sauce

Cut core out of the cabbage and gently remove leaves whole. Steam leaves until limp enough to be flexible, then allow to cool. Steam rice. When the rice is tender and still hot, add cheese, spices, and butter, margarine or ghee. Mix well.

When cabbage and rice mixture are cool enough to handle comfortably, spoon rice mixture into the cabbage leaves and roll up, tucking the ends in to prevent spillage. Place rolls in greased baking pan, and cover liberally with tomato sauce. Bake at 375° for 30-40 minutes, or until cabbage is completely tender.

Stuffed Cabbage Casserole

Stuffed rolls are more pleasing to the eye and the flavors are more distinct, but if you're in a hurry, just make a casserole. Cut cabbage into squares, mix ingredients, and bake as above.

Fettuccini

Use homemade noodles if possible.

1 recipe noodle dough, cut in ¼" inch wide noodles,
or 1 pound dried noodles
¾ cup butter
¾ cup grated fresh Parmesan cheese
½ cup heavy cream
salt and pepper to taste

Cook noodles *al dente* (Italian, meaning, *to the teeth,* or in other words, as done as you like it while still having some body). Drain. While noodles are boiling, cream the Parmesan in the butter. Beat in the cream. Toss the noodles with the sauce until thoroughly coated.

Avocado Casserole

2 cups cooked rice
2 stalks celery
1 can tomatoes, drained and quartered
4 avocados, peeled and diced
1 16-ounce tub sour cream
1 teaspoon lemon juice
1 cup bread crumbs
butter sufficient for sautéing
1 cup mozzarella cheese

1 cup cottage cheese
½ cup milk
2 teaspoon flour
salt and pepper to taste
½ teaspoon oregano
½ teaspoon cumin

Steam rice. Peel and dice avocados, sprinkling with lemon juice to retard discoloration. Sauté celery and mix together with rice and tomatoes. Make a roux (see page 212) with cheese, milk, flour, and spices. Sauté bread crumbs in butter. Beginning with the cooked rice, layer the avocado, roux, and breadcrumbs in a 13 x 9 baking pan. Bake at 350° for 15-20 minutes, just long enough to heat through.

To make this recipe without dairy, substitute ½ cup soy milk, 1 ½ cups soy mayonnaise, and 2 teaspoons flour or egg substitute for two eggs.

Optional: Add ¼ to ½ teaspoon sugar if desired.

Cheese Stuffed Zucchini

2 medium zucchini
¼ cup chopped celery
½ cup chopped apple
½ pound cooked sausage tofu (page 83)
2 slices day-old bread, toasted, cubed
1 cup grated Mozzarella cheese
lemon, basil or other Italian herbs, to taste

Boil zucchini in water for five minutes. Drain and cool. Cut in half lengthwise. Scoop out pulp leaving ¼ inch shell. Chop pulp. In skillet, add sausage tofu, zucchini pulp, celery, and apple. Cook until tender. Remove from heat, toss in bread cubes, and mix until moist.

Add ¼ cup cheese and mix thoroughly. Sprinkle the inside of the zucchini shells with lemon and herb spice. Stuff shells with zucchini mixture and place in baking pan. Bake 350° for 25 to 30 minutes. Top with remaining cheese, return to oven and bake only until cheese melts. Humm, good.

Rice Spinach Pie

This dish was a new taste for me when I first became a vegetarian. It helped confirm that "rabbit food" was delicious.

- 4 eggs or egg substitute (or use 1 pound fresh, soft tofu)
- 2 cups cooked rice
- ⅔ cup finely grated Swiss cheese
- 1 10-ounce package chopped spinach or fresh spinach
- 2 teaspoons butter
- 2 cups cottage cheese
- 6 teaspoons heavy cream or evaporated milk
- ¼ teaspoon nutmeg
- ½ teaspoon salt

Beat 1 egg or substitute, or blend tofu until smooth. Add rice and Swiss cheese. Stir mixture well then spread evenly in greased 9 inch pie pan for crust. Refrigerate. Press out all liquid from spinach, add butter, and set aside. In medium bowl, beat 3 eggs or substitute (or blend tofu until smooth). Stir in salt, cottage cheese, cream, and nutmeg. When well blended, stir in spinach, then pour into rice crust. Bake 350° for 30 to 35 minutes or until knife comes out clean. Serve in wedges.

Zucchini Frittata

2 teaspoons salad oil
2 large Swiss chard leaves (including stems) or spinach, coarsely chopped
1 medium zucchini, coarsely chopped
6 eggs or substitute, or 1 pound soft tofu, blended until smooth
¼ teaspoon dry basil
¼ teaspoon oregano leaves
1 cup grated Parmesan cheese
salt and pepper to taste

Sauté chard and zucchini for about 5 minutes. (If using spinach, add in the final minute of sautéing.) Beat eggs or substitutes with spices and blend into tofu. Stir in cheese and veggies. Pour into greased 9-inch pie pan. Bake at 350° for 25-30 minutes, or until puffed and brown.

Baked Eggplant

Almost any recipe can be changed to work for vegetarians. This one is modified from a cafeteria recipe that included meat.

1 pound eggplant, peeled
½ pound dry bread, cubed
½ cup milk
¼ cup butter, melted
¼ cup green peppers, finely chopped
¼ cup celery, finely chopped
2 eggs, or substitutes, slightly beaten
1 teaspoons salt
½ teaspoon pepper
¼ teaspoon sage
1 ½ cups (4 ounces) cheddar cheese, grated

Cut peeled eggplant into 1-inch cubes, soak in salt water in refrigerator overnight (minimum six hours, to remove any bitterness). Drain eggplant and place in pan. Cover with water and simmer until tender. Soak bread cubes in milk. Sauté green peppers and celery in melted butter.

Combine cooked eggplant, bread cubes, and sautéed vegetables. Add eggs or substitutes, pimento, and seasonings; mix thoroughly. Place in greased baking dish and bake at 350° for 45 minutes. Remove from oven, top with grated cheese, and return to oven until cheese melts.

Tomatoes Stuffed with Rice and Cheese

4 large tomatoes
1 cup (½ pound) cheddar, shredded
2 cups rice, cooked
3 tablespoons oil
1 tablespoon lemon juice
¼ teaspoon black pepper
butter

Cut a slice from the top of each tomato then scoop out pulp, leaving the shell. Remove the seeds and chop remaining pulp. Combine with ¾ cup of cheese, cooked rice, oil, lemon juice, and pepper. Stuff tomatoes with mixture, so that rice mounds over the top. Top with dots of butter and remaining cheese. Bake at 400° for 20 to 25 minutes.

To create **Mediterranean-Style Baked Tomatoes**, mix chopped tomatoes, parsley and bread crumbs, sprinkle with Romano and olive oil, bake uncovered for 1 hour at 350°.

Tamale Corn Pudding

2 tablespoons olive oil
½ green pepper, seeded and chopped
1 large tomato, peeled and chopped.
1 cup cream-style corn
1 cup boiling water
1 teaspoon salt
2 tablespoon chili powder (page 227 or store-bought)
½ cup sliced pitted ripe olives
½ pound soft Monterey Jack or mild cheddar, cubed

Sauté green pepper and tomato in olive oil until soft; combine with corn, corn meal, boiling water, salt and chili powder. Blend well. Turn into greased casserole dish, add olives and cheese, and stir to mix lightly. Bake at 375° until firm and lightly browned.

CHAPTER 11
Sources of Protein: Nuts and Seeds

"I didn't know nuts could be used that way!"

Until I became a vegetarian, I thought nuts were for Christmas or party trays. I had no idea that they give almost any dish an unexpected kick of flavor. For instance, English walnuts make quick gourmet fare of pasta when scattered over the top along with sautéed mixed vegetables like broccoli, julienned carrots, and multi-colored sliced peppers, chopped fresh basil, lemon pepper and Feta cheese. The result is a dish I fell in love with when I first ate it in a fancy restaurant.

There are many more types of nuts and recipes for them than I can squeeze into the space in this book, so you might want to see what other recipes you can find. As delicious and high in protein as nuts are, they really should be used more frequently. Seeds are another under-used food. They add interest and variety as well as nutrition.

Sunny Seed Salad

This is so easy. Pour a 16-ounce tub of cottage cheese into a bowl, add a can of crushed pineapple, throw in a handful of sunflower seeds, mix well and—presto—instant low-fat lunch.

Almond Soup

2 tablespoons butter
2 tablespoons flour
4 cups vegetable stock
½ cup ground almonds
½ cup heavy cream
salt and pepper to taste

Simmer 10 minutes.

Rice Pilaf with Pine Nuts

4 tablespoons ghee
¼ teaspoon allspice
2 cups rice, cooked
2 cups vegetable stock
½ cup pine nuts, toasted
salt and pepper to taste

In a skillet fry the rice with butter and spices until well cooked. Add remaining ingredients except nuts, bring to a boil, then cover, simmer 20 minutes. Add nuts before serving.

Tofu Stuffing with Pine Nuts and Raisins

1 box soft tofu
¾ cup breadcrumbs
½ cup vegetable stock
½ cup toasted pine nuts, chopped
½ cup raisins
½ teaspoon cinnamon
2 medium apples, cored and sliced
butter, salt and pepper to taste

Soak bread in vegetable stock. Mix ingredients and place in 13 x 9 baking dish. Bake at 375° for 30 minutes.

Tofu in Tomato Sauce with Almonds and Pine Nuts

½ cup olive oil
2 cups fresh or canned tomatoes, chopped
½ cup ground blanched almonds
⅓ cup pine nuts
1 pounds chopped parsley
2 cups tofu, cubed small

Grind almonds and pine nuts in blender with 3 tablespoons water. Stir in tomato sauce. Cook five minutes.

Carrot-Walnut Patties

1 pound sliced, steamed carrots
1 egg or substitute
2 tablespoons flour
½ teaspoon sugar
¼ cup chopped walnuts
salt and pepper to taste

Put all ingredients except walnuts into blender, then mix the walnuts into the mixture. Cook in spoonfuls in medium-hot 375° skillet until brown, flattening the mix into patties.

Avocado on the Half Shell, with Sunny Seeds

4 large ripe avocados (ripe meaning they just yield to thumb pressure)
½ cup sunflower seeds
½ cup chopped celery
½ green pepper
1 teaspoon lemon juice
4 to 8 ounces sour cream
6 ounces tofu; optional

Cut avocado in half. Dice one half, save the other for stuffing. Sauté or lightly steam veggies and tofu. In blender, combine sunflower seeds and spices, blend to fine powder; then combine with avocado, veggies, and tofu. Spoon into shell. Warm through in 350° oven for about ten minutes. Cover with sprigs of parsley. Add salt, pepper or any favorite spices.

Hazelnut Fritters

1 ½ cup flour
2 tablespoons sugar
¼ teaspoon cloves
½ teaspoon nutmeg
1 tablespoon grated orange rind
2 eggs or substitutes
¾ cups toasted ground hazelnuts
2 tablespoons confectioners' (powdered) sugar

Mix ingredients except for confectioners' sugar, drop by teaspoons into 350° oil, and fry until golden brown. Roll in confectioners' sugar.

Broccoli and Tomatoes with Sunny Seeds

½ head broccoli broken into florets (or large zucchini, sliced or cubed), and steamed
2 cups cooked rice
1 16-ounce can tomatoes, quartered and drained
2 tablespoons butter
½ teaspoon marjoram
½ teaspoon basil
½ teaspoon cumin
1 teaspoon salt
¼ teaspoon pepper
½ cup sunflower or sesame seeds

Steam vegetables. If you have time, it adds flavor to sauté the seeds and herbs in butter before mixing with the veggies. Otherwise, cook veggies then add remaining ingredients and serve.

Rice With Dates and Almonds

2 cups rice, cooked
¾ cup blanched almonds, halved
8 tablespoons butter
½ cup raisins
¼ pound dates, chopped
½ cup water

Steam the rice. As it cooks, sauté almonds in 4 tablespoons butter until just golden. Add raisins, dates, and water and simmer for 15 minutes or until dates are soft and water has been absorbed. Mix with hot rice and add remaining butter.

Millet Nut Loaf

Millet is a heavier grain but is has an interesting flavor and this recipe works really well for it.

1 cup uncooked millet
2 ½ cups water
2 tablespoons butter
1 can tomatoes, drained, chopped
¼ teaspoon sage
½ teaspoon rosemary
½ teaspoon thyme
1 sliced carrot
2 stalks celery, sliced
½ cup sunflower seeds
¼ cup sesame seeds
½ cup sliced almonds
salt to taste

Boil water. Add millet, vegetables, and spices. Return to boil, stirring once. Cover and lower temperature to slow simmer. Cook for 30 minutes. Add nuts and seeds. Serve.

Lentil Nut Loaf

1 small green pepper, chopped fine
3 tablespoons oil
½ cup wheat germ
2 cups lentils, cooked and drained
½ cup bread crumbs
½ cup sunflower seed or walnut pieces
½ teaspoon sage or thyme
2 eggs or egg substitute
2 tablespoons flour
½ cup vegetable stock or water
1 tablespoon lemon juice
sesame seeds

Sauté green pepper in oil until soft. Mix ingredients and place in greased loaf pan. Sprinkle generously with sesame seeds. Cover with aluminum foil or parchment and bake at 350° for 30 minutes. Uncover and continue baking for ten minutes.

Savory Dinner Loaf

1 cup bulgur wheat, cooked
1 cup soy grits, cooked
½ cup sesame or sunflower seeds, ground
1 ⅔ cups bread crumbs
2 eggs, or substitute, beaten
2 tablespoons oil
1 to 2 cups tomato sauce
2 cups vegetables, cooked and chopped
1 teaspoon salt
½ teaspoon sage
¼ teaspoon pepper

Mix all ingredients, reserving ½ cup sauce for topping. Place mixture into a well greased 9 x 5 loaf pan and bake at 350° for 1 hour. Let stand 15 minutes before serving.

CHAPTER 12
Grains

The Forgotten Staff of Nutrition

Until I became a vegetarian, all I knew about grains was that they were in the white stuff that one put meat patties between (i.e. bread) or the flaky stuff that came out of a box for breakfast that one poured milk over. Sure, I'd had Grandma's delicious cooked oatmeal, but it never occurred to me that it would be used for any meal except breakfast. Except fried rice at the Mexican place, I thought rice was for breakfast too, with sugar and raisins. It never thought of any grain as a food item to be eaten for its own sake or as a main dish.

As I grew in vegetarian savvy, I discovered that grains are not only high in fiber and nutrients, there were about a million interesting things you can do with them, including allow their taste to be neutral. In the East, rice is often used intentionally as a backdrop to the food. The bland flavor is used to cleanse the palate between bites of more heavily flavored foods.

If you are new to grains, you might try what one family with six kids did—looking for cost-effective foods, they experimented with unfamiliar grains using butter, spices, sugar, honey, soy sauce, ketchup, or whatever tastes the kids wanted to try next. Sure enough, they learned to like them. Personally, I think the best way to learn to enjoy grains is to try the recipes in this chapter.

Cooking Chart for Grains
(per cup of grain)

Bring water to a boil then add grains while stirring.

Grain	Water	Cooking Time	Yield
Barley	3 cups	10-12 minutes	3 cups
Buckwheat (kasha)	2 cups	15 minutes	3 cups
Bulgur (wheat)	2 cups	15-20 minutes	2 ½ cups
Couscous	1 cups	5 minutes	1 ¼ cup
Millet	3 cups	45 minutes	3 ½ cups
Cornmeal	4 cups	25 minutes	3 cups
Rice (white)	2 cups	20 minutes	3 cups
Wild Rice	3 cups	1 hour (or more)	4 cups
Whole Wheat Berries	3 cups	2 hours	2 ⅔ cups

White Rice, Perfect Every Time

2 cups water
1 cup rice
1 tablespoon butter
salt optional

Bring water to a boil. Add washed rice. Stir two or three times, and cover with tight-fitting lid. Turn heat down to lowest and steam for 20 minutes. For softer rice, add an extra tablespoon of water.

Rule of Tongue for Rice: Stirring during cooking causes rice to become sticky.

White Rice Pudding

1 cup rice, cooked
2 tablespoons honey
½ cup raisins
1 ½ cup milk
¼ teaspoon cinnamon
1 teaspoon vanilla
nutmeg to taste

Combine all ingredients except honey and vanilla in the top of a double boiler. Place over water at a low boil, stirring occasionally, for 15 minutes to ½ hour. When cooled enough to eat, add honey and vanilla. Garnish with grated nutmeg.

Brown Rice or White Rice, That is the Question

Some say that because it has been hulled, white rice has little nutrition. Because of this many people believe that the unhulled brown rich is the better choice. However, Ayur Veda says the husk makes it too hard to digest.

After trying both, my choice was to defer to the wisdom of many generations of Orientals who have thrived on white rice. The "trick" is to use the good stuff. A rice of choice is Basmati, a plump, nutty-tasting grain which a rice lover can identify by taste. It's sometimes called Eastern or Jasmine rice. A U.S. version is called Texmati rice.

As always, organic is best, especially because there is even less regulation of pesticides outside the US.

Sharalyn Pliler

Rice Pilaf

2 cups rice, cooked (or other grain, such as millet, bulgar or couscous)
1 cup peas
1 cup black olives
1 tablespoon olive oil
¼ teaspoon turmeric
1 teaspoon salt
¼ teaspoon pepper

Mix cooked rice with other ingredients and place in greased 13 x 9 baking pan. Bake at 375° for 30 minutes or until warmed.

Veggie Rice

2 cups rice, cooked
1 cup steamed broccoli
¼ cup fresh parsley, chopped
1 cup cut-up canned or fresh tomatoes
1 teaspoon thyme
butter to taste

Mix, heat through, and serve.

Pulao (Peas and Rice)

1 cup uncooked rice
2 cups water
2 teaspoons butter
½ teaspoon cumin
½ teaspoon ginger
½ teaspoon turmeric
1 cup cooked peas
salt and pepper to taste

Sauté uncooked rice in butter. Add water and spices, bring to a boil, cover and lower heat to lowest setting; cook for 20 minutes. When rice is tender, add peas and heat through.

Spanish Rice

1 cup rice
2 cups water or stock
2 tablespoons butter
1 (16-ounce) can tomatoes, cut up
½ cup diced green peppers
1 can black olives
2 whole cloves
1 teaspoon oregano
½ teaspoon basil
1 small bay leaf
pinch sugar

Sauté rice, green peppers, and spices in butter. Add water or stock, bring to a boil, cover and reduce heat. Simmer 20 minutes. Add olives and tomatoes and heat through.

Rice with Carrots

1 to 1 ½ carrots, coarsely grated
2 tablespoons sugar
½ teaspoon ground cinnamon
2 cups cooked rice
salt to taste
butter

Steam rice. Sauté carrots in butter. Spread alternate layers of rice and carrots in heavy, buttered pan, cover and cook over low heat for 30 minutes. To make this an authentic Mid-

Eastern dish, sprinkle 1 tablespoon rose water over the top. This dish works well served with tofu meat balls.

Rice Broccoli Casserole

1 cup rice, cooked
3 cups broccoli, cut into florets
5 ounces cheddar cheese, shredded
1 cup of cream sauce (page 199)
¼ cup butter

Mix ingredients and place in oiled casserole dish. Bake at 350° for 30 to 40 minutes, or until broccoli is tender.

Bachelor's Rice and Lentils

I had a bachelor friend who swore by this recipe, pointing out that it is simple, nutritious, quick, and cost-effective. Before he got married, he had it for supper at least 6 nights a week. After he got married, despite his protests, his wife reduced it to 2 or 3 times a week.

For one serving:

1 ounce rice
1 ounce lentils
2 ounces water
1 teaspoon curry powder
1 ounce cheddar cheese, shredded

Place all ingredients except cheese into pan. Bring to a boil, stir once and cover with tight-fitting lid, reduce heat, and simmer for 30 minutes. Add cheese to hot mixture. Serve with soy sauce.

For variety, add carrots, green peppers, or other vegetables.

Buckwheat: Kasha

1 egg or substitute, beaten
1 ½ cups coarse buckwheat groats (ask for these at your local health food store)
3 to 4 cups boiling water
1 small green pepper, diced
2 tablespoons vegetable oil

Add egg or substitute to groats and mix well. Place in skillet over medium heat and cook until groats are dry and toasty. Add 3 cups boiling water gradually, while stirring. Cover, reduce heat, and cook for 15 minutes, or until tender. Add more water if kasha begins to dry out. Sauté green pepper in oil and add to cooked kasha.

Millet: Stuffed Peppers

4 green peppers, halved lengthwise
1 tablespoon vegetable oil
½ pound tofu hamburger, prepared
½ cup millet, cooked
2 tablespoons fresh parsley, chopped
1 teaspoon oregano
1 tablespoon soy sauce
2 tablespoons wheat germ
2 tablespoons grated Parmesan cheese
1 ½ cups tomato sauce, warmed

Combine tofu hamburger with millet, herbs, and soy sauce and spoon into pepper halves. Place stuffed pepper in a large shallow baking pan and bake at 350° for 1 hour. Sprinkle tops with wheat germ and cheese for final 20 minutes of baking.

Couscous

Couscous (or cous cous) is the traditional dish of Morocco, Algeria and Tunisia. Actually a type of pasta, it cooks in seconds. Serve it with vegetables and seasonings or as a main or side dish for dinner. It is also a good grain for a fast-fix hot breakfast—just add butter and sweet.

1 cup couscous
1 ¼ cup water, boiling
3 tablespoons butter
salt if desired

Add couscous, butter, and salt to boiling water. Remove from heat and allow to stand for 5 minutes. Stir to fluff up.

Carob Couscous Pudding

From Fantastic Foods Company, which makes a lot of vegetarian products.

3 cups milk
4 tablespoons toasted carob powder (or cocoa)
⅓ cup sugar
2 tablespoons butter
1 teaspoon almond extract
¼ teaspoon cardamom
½ cup whipping cream

Blend milk, carob powder and sugar until smooth. Heat to simmer, stirring frequently. Add butter and couscous, simmer and stir with wire whisk until thick (10 to 12 minutes for carob, less for cocoa). Remove from heat, add almond extract and cardamom. Cool. Blend until smooth. Whip cream and fold into pudding. Refrigerate covered for several hours. Garnish with slivers of toasted almonds.

Couscous with Peas

2 cups vegetable stock
1 stick butter, cut in small pieces
1 teaspoon cumin
¼ teaspoon cayenne pepper
1 ½ cups cooked fresh peas or 1 (10-ounce) package frozen peas, thawed
2 cups couscous
2 tablespoons fresh cilantro, minced or 3 tablespoons fresh parsley leaves
salt and pepper to taste

In a saucepan bring the broth, butter, cumin and cayenne to a boil. Stir in peas and Couscous, cover and turn off heat. Allow to stand for four minutes. Add cilantro or parsley and serve.

Other gains include rye, semolina, spelt, amarant, kamut, quinoa, sorghum, and triticale. To experiment with these different but delicious tastes without buying a whole box or bag, you can purchase small amounts from the bulk section of your local health food store, inquiring from how to cook these grains.

CHAPTER 13
Breads and Baking

"Look Mom, no eggs!"

For many years, I had an allergy to dairy products. In learning to cook without milk and eggs, I rediscovered that *what seems like a loss often turns out to be a gain*. Here's an example. Diners at my table frequently raved about my biscuits and cornbread. I gladly accepted the compliments but I had no idea why they were so outstanding until the day I served biscuits to two elderly guests, my friend Kay (who was a great cook in her own right), and Edna.

"Why, I don't think I have ever eaten such good biscuits," Edna exclaimed. "The texture is so light and flaky."

Kay, who had weeks earlier gotten the recipe from me, leaned toward Edna with a conspiratorial look. "You'll never guess what she puts in them," she said. Then, with a dramatic pause and a smug look, she gave out the "secret." (I listened carefully so I'd know too.)

"Water!" she exclaimed. "She uses water, not milk."

I have since tried both ways and discovered that Kay was right. Water creates a crispier texture which everyone seems to love.

So, let's throw away old expectations of how things are *supposed* to taste or what ingredients *must* be used. Instead, let's think outside the lunch box. For instance, what gives cake its lightness? Eggs, of course. The more eggs and the longer they are beaten, the lighter the cake. So what do those of us who don't eat eggs do for cake? The answer is simple—we learn to bake cakes that don't need eggs, or we use egg alternatives. The result is different, but different turns out to be delicious.

Eggless Cakes

According to Miriam Kasin, author of *Heaven's Banquet,* eggs do four things in baking: They provide:

- **Liquids**. Liquids can of course easily be replaced with water, milk, milk substitute, tea or virtually any edible liquid.
- **Leavening** (raising) is provided by combining the usual amounts of baking powder or baking soda, with sour milk, buttermilk, yogurt, or sour cream, mixed ½ with water. (These dairy products actually work better for leavening than the sweet milk called for in most recipes.)
- **Binding,** which can be achieved with egg substitutes from the grocery or health food store, or with Kasin's recipe for binding powder (see box on the following page.)
- **Lightness** is the most challenging. To make light cakes without eggs, try using the tips in the box.

You can also purchase egg substitutes at the grocery and health food stores, such as EnerG Foods Egg Replacer.

Tips for Making Light Cakes without Eggs

- *Mix batter only enough to blend all the ingredients. Kasin says, "Overbeating develops glucyness." It becomes gluey because it increases the gluten in the flour and toughens the mixture.*
- *Creaming the butter and sugar together before preparing batter adds lightness.*
- *Using unbleached flour helps to create lightness. Bleached flours rise unevenly.*
- *For greater lightness and smooth, even rising, use a mix of half white flour and half whole-wheat flour.*
- *The use of baking soda as part of the leavening "tenderizes" the batter.*
- *In biscuits and cornbread, water serves to produce a crisper product, but to get light cakes diary is almost essential. If you do not wish to use dairy products at all, you might find the best solution is to switch to fruit-based cakes such as Ranch Apple on page 135.*

More tips on cooking without Eggs and Dairy

- *Béchamel sauce, mashed potatoes, sour cream, tahini, and nut butters all help hold foods together.*
- *Replace the ¼ cup of liquid the egg provides with water or milk, or leave it out entirely as most eggless cakes need less liquid anyway*

Miriam Kasin's Binding Powder

½ cup soy flour
½ cup arrowroot or cornstarch.

Store in closed jar. Use 2 tablespoons for one egg. (This is enough to bind a standard cake).

Note: Oat flour and potato flour may also be used.

Cakes

Sour Cream Spice Cake

From Miriam Kasin's *The Age of Enlightenment Cookbook*

½ cup butter
2 cups packed brown sugar
1 ½ cups sour cream
½ cup water
3 cups unbleached white flour
½ cup whole wheat flour
3 tablespoons Binding Powder (see above)
1 teaspoon ground coffee powder
½ teaspoon salt
1 ½ teaspoon baking powder
1 teaspoon soda
1 ½ teaspoon cinnamon
½ teaspoon each: cloves, ground ginger, nutmeg, cardamom

Cream butter and sugar. Add sour cream and beat until smooth. Add the water. Sift dry ingredients into the sour cream mixture. Mix just until blended. Pour into 2 buttered floured 8-inch cake pans and bake at 350° about 35 minutes. Makes two 8-inch layers.

Mexican Surprise Cake

This is my mother's favorite cake recipe and the family never gets tired of it. You probably won't get tired of it either.

- 2 cups flour
- 1 cup sugar
- 2 eggs or egg substitute
- 1 ½ teaspoons soda
- 1 (20-ounce) can crushed pineapple, undrained
- ½ cup pecans

Mix together flour, sugar, eggs, and soda, and then add pineapple, pecans, and one teaspoon flavoring in large bowl. Mix until just-blended. Pour into 13 x 9 pan (ungreased). Bake at 350° for one hour, or until cake tests done in the middle.

Frosting: Blend 1 stick melted butter or margarine, 2 cups powdered sugar, 8 ounces cream cheese, and (optional) 1 teaspoon black walnut flavoring. Beat until well-mixed. Spread over warm cake.

Ranch Apple Cake

Be ready to give out this recipe—everyone loves it. This is my favorite eggless cake.

- 1 cup flour
- ¾ cup sugar
- ¼ teaspoon baking soda
- ½ teaspoon salt
- ½ cup salad oil

2 eggs or substitute
1 teaspoon cinnamon
2 cups apples, chopped fine
½ cup chopped walnuts
½ cup raisins

Mix dry ingredients; add oil, apple, eggs or substitute, nuts, and raisins. Stir well and pour into greased 8 x 8 square pan. Bake at 325° for 45 minutes to one hour.

Note: The Ranch Apple Cake recipe came originally from a pamphlet of recipes from Sterling Foods Company. Sterling makes "Special Blend Flour," a tasty mixture that some people with wheat allergies have been able to tolerate.

Tofu Cheesecake

Does a vegetarian have to give up decadent tastes? Absolutely not. Here's a marvelous favorite dessert that even the most strict vegan will be able to eat with both a clear conscience and lip-smacking pleasure.

2 pounds fresh soft tofu
½ teaspoon salt
¼ cup lemon juice
½ cup oil
½ cup sugar
2 teaspoons vanilla
1 tablespoon corn starch

Dissolve cornstarch in 2 tablespoons water. Combine with remaining filling ingredients and blend until creamy.

To make crust, crush 8-ounces of graham cracker crumbs, mix with ¾ cup butter or margarine, softened, then press into a 9-inch pie tine. Pour in filling and bake at 375° for 40 minutes or until top is golden brown and cheesecake has jelled. Top with fruit if desired. Chill 2 hours before serving.

Pies

Impossible Pie

No crust needed. This is another recipe I got from my mother.

¾ cup sugar
½ cup flour
½ teaspoon baking powder
¼ teaspoon salt
¼ teaspoon cloves
¼ teaspoon ginger
¼ teaspoon allspice
½ teaspoon cinnamon
1 tablespoon vegetable oil
2 tablespoons butter
1 ½ cups milk, or nut milk
1 can pumpkin or 1 cup cooked fresh pumpkin
2 eggs or egg substitutes
1 ½ teaspoons vanilla

Mix dry ingredients, add remaining ingredients, smooth. Pour into greased 9- or 10-inch pan. Bake at 350° F for 50 to 55 minutes.

Lorraine's Wonderful Pumpkin Pie

1 can pumpkin or 1 cup fresh cooked pumpkin
1 egg or egg substitute
¾ cup sugar
1 ½ cups milk or milk substitute
1 heaping tablespoon flour
¼ teaspoon salt

¼ teaspoon cloves
¼ teaspoon ginger
¼ teaspoon allspice
½ teaspoon cinnamon

Beat egg or egg substitute into pumpkin. Mix dry ingredients and add to pumpkin mixture. Beat smooth, pour into pie shell and bake at 400° F for 20 to 30 minutes, reduce heat to 325° F and continue baking for 1 hour.

Breads

Prize-Winning Zucchini Bread

This recipe was given to me handwritten by a friend so I don't know who won the prize for it. Whoever it was, he or she certainly deserved it. Try this and see if you don't agree.

3 tablespoons butter (soft)
1 cup sugar
2 eggs or substitute
1 tablespoon grated orange rind (amazing how much zing a little thing like fresh orange rind adds)
1 (16-ounce) can whole berry cranberry sauce
1 1/ 2 cups all purpose flour
1 ½ cups whole wheat flour
1 teaspoon baking soda
2 teaspoons baking powder
1 ½ cup grated zucchini
1 cup walnuts, chopped

Heat oven to 350°. Grease and flour two 8 x 4 baking pans. In a medium bowl, beat butter, sugar and eggs (or egg substitute) until fluffy. Stir in orange rind and cranberry sauce. Measure flour, baking soda, and baking powder into butter mixture, fold in until combined, then fold in zucchini and walnuts. Turn into pans. Bake until toothpick inserted comes out clean, about 1 ½ hours, or 1 hour for small pans. Cool before slicing.

Biscuits

Biscuits made without milk have a light, crispy texture, which you may like even better than biscuits made with milk.

2 cups sifted flour
2 ½ teaspoons baking powder
1 teaspoon salt
⅓ cup shortening or butter
⅔ cup water or milk

Sift together dry ingredients. Cut in shortening or butter until consistency of coarse meal. Stir in enough water or milk to make a soft dough. Round up on lightly floured surface and knead gently. Roll out one-half thickness desired in finished biscuits. Cut with floured cutter, place on ungreased baking sheet. Bake in 450° oven 12 to 15 minutes.

Note: To turn biscuit into shortcake, decrease shortening to ⅓ cup and add 2 tablespoons of sugar.

Cornbread

Guests nearly always mention how good my cornbread is, but all I do that is different from the recipe on packaged cornmeal is to use water instead of milk, and egg substitute instead of eggs, or no eggs at all. Cornbread without eggs is crumblier and crunchier, which you may like better.

1 cup cornmeal
1 cup flour

¼ cup sugar
4 teaspoons baking powder
1 teaspoon salt
1 cup water or milk
¼ cup oil

Mix dry ingredients. Add remaining ingredients, mix only long enough to moisten, then pour into a greased 9″ baking pan. Bake 425 °F for 20 minutes or until the crust is light golden brown.

Quick Cornbread Tip

To decrease preparation time, dry ingredients for cornbread can be mixed ahead of time so they're always handy. Multiply recipe amounts of dry ingredients by 4, mix well, and store in a large jar or sealed can. To use, measure out 2 cups plus 2 tablespoons of mixture, then add 1 cup water or milk and ¼ cup oil, then mix and bake according to recipe.

CHAPTER 14
Making Vegetables Sing

"Delicious!"

If you're still feeling some reluctance or uncertainty about vegetables, go back and reread Chapter 5. Remember, fresh is the most important aspect of vegetables. Choose vegetables as fresh as you can get them, preferably organic, local if possible, and best of all, straight out of your own garden. Wash thoroughly, don't overcook, and remember to experiment.

Rules of Tongue for Vegetables:

To steam or to boil, that is the question:

Steaming preserves the nutrients, boiling preserves the color. Now you have to choose your personal preference. One way to get both is to boil or simmer, then drink the "pot liquor"—the broth—directly from a cup, use it as soup stock, or mix it into other dishes. Pot liquor from kale or chard is especially good.

Degree of doneness:

Many people find that crisper veggies taste more flavorful, but longer cooking makes food more digestible. You choose what works best for you.

Now, here are some vegetable recipes that vegetable lovers will love ... and those who *think* they don't love vegetables will love.

Four Seasons Casserole

This vegetable casserole can be made anytime with whatever fresh vegetables you have available. For a base, use cottage cheese or a white sauce (page 212) with hard cheeses such as cheddar, mozzarella, or Monterey jack. To add even add more nutrients, zest and heartiness toss in sunflower seeds, water chestnuts, or frozen peas. Be creative. Begin by following this classic recipe then customize it to delight your particular taste buds. With cheeses, this can serve as your protein main dish.

1 ½ cup broccoli (or cauliflower or eggplant), cut into florets or cubed
1 medium zucchini, sliced or cubed
1 (16-ounce) can tomatoes, drained and quartered
2 cups cooked grain (rice or barley)
2 cups cottage cheese
1 teaspoon marjoram
¼ teaspoon celery seed
2 tablespoons butter
salt and pepper to taste

Mix ingredients. Place in an oiled 13 x 9 baking pan. Dot with butter. Sprinkle with bread crumbs if desired. Bake at 350° for 1 hour, or until veggies are tender and cheese has melted.

Stir-Fries

What you put in stir-fries depends upon your taste and whatever fresh vegetables are available. Experiment until you find the combination that suits your individual taste buds. Start with classic Oriental vegetables such as Chinese cabbage, bok choy, and snow peas. Serve with rice or noodles and sweet-and-sour sauce.

⅓ head of broccoli, broken into florets
3 carrots, sliced thin
¼ head of cabbage, cut into 1-inch squares
2 ribs celery, sliced
1 green pepper, sliced or cut into chunks
1 pound fresh or frozen (and thawed) tofu, well drained, diced
1 can sliced water chestnuts, drained
½ cup sunflower seeds
½ teaspoon cinnamon
1 teaspoon grated fresh ginger

Traditional: Place broccoli in hot skillet or wok with small amount of oil. Sprinkle cinnamon over broccoli. Stir constantly to prevent burning, 3 to 4 minutes. Remove and set aside. Add more oil if necessary, then add carrots. Sprinkle carrots with ginger and stir/fry 3 to 4 minutes. Remove, set aside, repeating with each vegetable, adding oil as needed to prevent sticking, and stirring to prevent scorching. Stir-fry sunflower seeds. Add 1 tablespoon of soy sauce to tofu and stir-fry. Mix all ingredients together. Serve with rice and sweet-and-sour sauce.

Quick: Those skilled in the art of cooking know that all foods should be prepared with unhurried love. But let's face it, most of the time, we're late for the next appointment. It would be nice if we could slow down but if you need to save time, stir-fries *can* be prepared quickly (in the time it takes the rice to steam). Add the veggies in the sequence they are listed in order to accommodate the cooking time requirements. Stir frequently to prevent scorching, adding a bit of water and covering if necessary to bring to desired tenderness. They won't be as perfect but if you use fresh ingredients, they will still taste delicious.

Vegetable Curry

Curried vegetables are lively, hearty, and simple. Take whatever vegetables you have on hand, cook them together, adding East Indian spices to taste, from strong to subtle. (You can buy curry mixes ready made or try the homemade curry recipe on page 226. You may also want to use the recipe for making your own ghee, or clarified butter, on page 216. Besides being good for you, ghee adds a special richness to the taste of curries.) Serve as is or add cubed tofu. With a little experimentation, you will find a combination that you will look forward to every time you cook.

2 tablespoons ghee
2 medium potatoes, cubed
2 green peppers, cut up
½ head cauliflower, cut into florets
1 cup peas
3 tomatoes, quartered, or 1 can tomatoes
½ tablespoon cilantro (coriander leaves) minced
½ teaspoon coriander seeds
½ tablespoon cumin
1 teaspoon fresh ginger, chopped fine
1 bay leaf
1 teaspoon salt, if desired
¼ teaspoon turmeric
¼ teaspoon black pepper
4 whole cloves

Heat ghee in skillet and sauté spices. Stir in potatoes and fry till brown. Add remaining ingredients and a cup of hot water. Simmer until vegetables are tender.

Note: Any vegetables may be added or substituted.

Potato Cabbage Curry

Curried Veggies can be as fancy or as simple as you wish. For a quick, easy and tasty dish, try sautéing potatoes, cabbage, zucchini, and celery together in ghee. Add curry and coriander to taste. (Try using 2 **teaspoons or more of coriander.) Add salt and pepper to taste, and cook until tender.**

English Pott

By Jove, those English folks certainly know how to prepare a hearty dish.

2 medium potatoes, cubed
2 stalks celery, sliced
2 medium carrots, sliced
1 cup frozen peas
1 cup cottage cheese
½ teaspoon parsley
¼ teaspoon thyme
½ teaspoon pepper
¼ teaspoon basil
2 tablespoons butter
salt to taste
1 cup bread crumbs

Mix all ingredients well and place in a greased 13 x 9 baking pan. Dot with butter. Sprinkle with bread crumbs. Bake at 400° for 1 hour, or until veggies are tender and the cheese melts.

Benarasi Cauliflower

Oooh, I love this dish. It has a lingering, unforgettable taste, a subtle zing for the palate.

Suggestion: double or triple the sauce recipe and freeze the extra portions for later use.

1 large cauliflower, divided into bite-sized florets
5 tablespoons ghee (page 216)
2 teaspoon ground coriander
¼ teaspoon ground turmeric
1 teaspoon salt
½ cup drained canned tomatoes with ½ cup of their liquid
½ teaspoon cumin
¼ teaspoon caraway seed
¼ teaspoon black peppercorns
2 whole cloves
2 cardamom pods, seeds only
1 bay leaf

Sauté the cauliflower in half the ghee until brown; set aside.

Purée the coriander, turmeric, salt, and tomatoes in a blender. Stir the purée into the ghee left in the casserole. Return the casserole to medium-low heat and cook, partially covered, for 10 minutes, or until the purée is reduced to a thick sauce. Stir constantly the last few minutes to prevent sticking.

Pulverize the cumin, caraway, peppercorns, cloves, cardamom and bay leaf in the blender, then stir them into the sauce. Fold in the reserved cauliflower until each piece is coated with sauce. Cover and bake in the pre-heated 350° oven for 1 hour, or until tender to preference.

Note: My experience has been that even though it seems logical to mix all the spices together, the tastes is much better if the recipe is followed exactly.

Stuffed Cabbage

Here's yet another recipe in which the flavors complements each other wonderfully. Nearly everyone who tries this dish asks for the recipe—even several who claimed to dislike cabbage.

1 medium head cabbage
2 cups rice, cooked
2 ½ cups shredded mozzarella and/or Muenster cheese
2 tablespoons caraway seed
¾ teaspoon salt
pepper to taste
2-3 tablespoons butter
1 (15-ounce) can tomato sauce

Cut the core out of the cabbage and gently remove the leaves, whole. Steam leaves until limp enough to be flexible, then allow to cool until they can be handled with comfort. Mix rice, cheese, and spices. Spoon the rice mixture into the cabbage leaves and roll up, tucking the ends in to prevent spillage. Place rolls in a 13 x 9 greased baking pan, and cover liberally with tomato sauce. Bake at 375° for 40 minutes, or until the cabbage is completely tender.

Stuffed Cabbage Casserole

Foods cooked with care taste better, but sometimes we don't have time to go for the best, so even though the rolled shapes in the recipe above are more aesthetically pleasing and the flavors more distinct, if you're in a hurry, the recipe above can be made as a casserole. Simply cut the cabbage into 1- or 2-inch squares and mix all ingredients together. Spoon into a greased baking pan. Bake at 375° for 1 hour or until leaves are tender.

Eggplant Fans

Eggplant is an admirable and versatile vegetable. If you have not acquired a taste for eggplant, it is probably because you haven't known to mix it with its best friends—olive oil, black olives, tomatoes, and basil. These tastes complement each other and the result is nutrient-rich, exotic-flavored dishes literally fit for kings and a wide range of taste bud preferences. To take out any bitter flavor, salt the peeled pieces of eggplant and let them drain in a colander for 30 minutes, then rinse with water and pat dry before cooking.

1 medium eggplant
1 large, firm tomato, sliced
2 cooked artichokes hearts (optional)
½ zucchini, sliced
½ cup small pitted black olives
⅓ to ½ cup olive oil
2 bay leaves, crumpled
¼ teaspoon thyme
¼ teaspoon oregano
¼ teaspoon savory
fresh basil leaves or ½ teaspoon dried basil

Split eggplant lengthwise. Cut each half lengthwise into ½-inch thickness, leaving the slices attached at the stem end to form fans. Arrange the eggplant halves, gently forced together, side by side in a baking dish in 2 tablespoons of olive oil. Stuff the crevices with zucchini, tomatoes, olives, and artichokes. Sprinkle with herbs and olive oil. Bake lightly covered for ten minutes at 450°, then about 1 ½ hours at 350°. When done, the stem ends of the eggplants should be soft to the touch. Serve either tepid or room temperature, sprinkled with fresh basil, with rice.

Grandma's Cooked Vegetable Salad

Carrots not only are good as a dish by themselves, almost any dish will welcome them for added body, color, flavor, and nutrients. This was one of my grandmother's favorite dishes, although she used onions instead of bok choy.

1 pound carrots, sliced
1 ½ cup home-made or canned tomato soup
½ cup sugar (optional)
1 bell pepper, chopped small
1 rib bok choy, chopped small
¼ cup lemon juice

Cook carrots, cool. Combine tomato soup, sugar and lemon juice, then mix with carrots. Serve at room temperature.

Other Carrot Ideas

Try carrots with:

- butter and honey
- lemon juice and sugar
- celery, almonds, lemon juice, and sugar
- pineapple, dill, sugar and butter
- parsley and sour cream

Parsnips

You probably have seen parsnips in the grocery store and wondered what to do with them. It's easy. Wash and scrape the same as with carrots, and slice. (Add some scrapped and sliced carrots too if you wish—carrots and parsnips like each other.) Sprinkle with nutmeg and sauté in butter until tender. Just see if it doesn't make you regret that you waited so long to try them.

Spinach with Artichoke Hearts

With this recipe, instead of having to beg your kids to eat their spinach, you may find they will be asking you, "Mom, can we have that spinach stuff for supper again?"

1 (5-ounce) can artichoke hearts
1 teaspoon butter
2 packages frozen chopped spinach, cooked,
  drained
8 ounce package cream cheese
1 teaspoon salt

½ teaspoon pepper
1 cup Swiss cheese, grated

In sauce pan, sauté artichokes in butter. Combine all ingredients except cheese, and pour into to a buttered 8-inch square baking dish. Top with cheese and bake at 350° for 30 minutes.

Tabouli Salad with Spinach

Tabouli is cracked Bulgar wheat, available in bulk or in boxed form. This favorite Mid-Eastern grain offers you great potential for creativity. To a basic recipe of tabouli, oil, lemon juice, and salt, add any favorite salad vegetables until you come up with your own favorite style. I like to chop the vegetables fine so it's more of a mix rather than a chunky salad.

1 cup tabouli, rinsed and drained
1 cup vegetable oil
1 cup lemon juice
4-6 cups fresh spinach, washed
1 cucumber
1 tomato
½ green pepper
parsley
salt to taste

Mix vegetables with other ingredients. Let stand in refrigerator overnight to allow flavors to blend.

Russian Borscht

Nobody likes beets, right? Wrong. This recipe for borscht—one of endless variations of a classic Russian soup that has been a mainstay for millions of people throughout history—just may inspire you to love beets too.

2 large beets, cubed
3 large potatoes, cubed
½ head of cabbage, chopped
1 rib celery, chopped
2 tablespoons butter
1 teaspoon sugar
salt to taste
parsley, chopped
black pepper, freshly ground, to taste
sour cream (or cottage cheese)

Simmer vegetables and seasonings in water until the vegetables are tender and the liquid is a rich red. Serve with garnish of parsley, fresh-grated black pepper, and a generous dollop of sour cream or cottage cheese.

Stuffed Tomatoes

Who doesn't love tomatoes? Here's a quick, easy recipe that pairs them with one of their favorite herbs, basil, mixed into a simple but elegant dressing that makes this dish good enough for guests any day.

4 large, medium ripe tomatoes
1 tablespoon olive oil
½ teaspoon basil (or 10-12 fresh basil leaves, minced)
¼ teaspoon black pepper
salt to taste, if desired
2 cups small pasta shells
¼ cup grated Parmesan cheese

Basil dressing

½ teaspoon basil (or 10-12 fresh basil leaves, minced)

2 tablespoons lemon juice
½ cup olive oil

Cook pasta shells. Spoon out contents of tomatoes and place in blender. Add spices and blend briefly. Mix blended tomato juice and pasta shells, and fill tomato shells. Cover with basil dressing and Parmesan cheese. Place tomatoes under a broiler and cook until the cheese is melted and lightly browned.

More Creative Vegetable Ideas

Tomatoes, squash, and **peppers** can be sliced lengthwise and spooned out to leave a channel for stuffing with any preferred combination of cheeses, rice, minced and sautéed vegetables, and bread crumbs, flavored with Italian and other herbs. Instant gourmet.

Zucchini Pizza

This recipe tells us that anyone who says vegetables aren't fun just hasn't been using any imagination.

4 cups zucchini, shredded
2 cups rice, cooked
1 ½ cup mozzarella cheese
1 ½ cup Parmesan cheese
2 eggs or substitute
1 (15-ounce) jar spaghetti sauce
1 green pepper, minced
(Optional: any other favorite, quick-cooking vegetable, minced or sliced thin)
1 teaspoon basil
1 teaspoon oregano

In a towel, squeeze the zucchini as dry as possible. Mix the zucchini, rice, 1 cup of each cheese, and eggs or substitute. Press mixture onto greased 15 x 10 baking pan. Bake at 400° for 15 minutes or until mixture is set and lightly browned. Remove from oven.

Mix spaghetti sauce, herbs, and peppers. Spoon mixture evenly over baked crust. Sprinkle with remaining cheeses. Bake in 400°oven 15 minutes, or until cheese melts. Let stand for 5 minutes, then cut into squares.

Okra Dokey

Many times people will taste a vegetable for the first time then immediately—and permanently—decide they don't like it. This happens frequently with okra because when it is boiled, it may seem too "slimy" for some tastes. However, it's fun to watch faces of those who claim to not like a particular veggie when they taste it cooked in a different way. Suddenly, they love it. This often happens with this recipe among those who claim to not like okra. Try it yourself and see if you don't agree that it's best to reserve judgments until you've had varied experiences.

2 cups fresh okra, sliced
1 rib celery, sliced
1 small zucchini, sliced
1 (16-ounce) can tomatoes, drained and cut up
½ teaspoon savory
½ teaspoon celery seed
¼ teaspoon pepper
Optional: ½ pound fresh or frozen (thawed) tofu, drained and chopped
vegetable oil as needed

Sauté okra, celery and zucchini in oil, with herbs and spices, to desired doneness. Add tomatoes and continue cooking until tomatoes are hot. Serve over rice.

Fried Okra

Okra can be sliced, rolled in flour, cornmeal, or a mixture of half-each flour and cornmeal, then fried or baked until browned. Crispy, crunchy, humm good.

Yam Apple Pie

In the U.S. many of us think of the sweet potato as special food to be eaten primarily at Thanksgiving, but in many countries, sweet potatoes are more common than what is in those countries called the "white" potato. Sweet potatoes are more digestible than white potatoes, and like white potatoes, can be used in many ways. They can be baked, fried, steamed, boiled, and baked in breads. (To bake: wash, pat dry, brush with butter, wrap in foil and bake at 425 ° for 1 ½ hours until tender.)

4 medium sweet potatoes
1 teaspoon cinnamon
½ teaspoon nutmeg
½ cup raisins
2 tablespoons butter
1 - 2 apples, cored and sliced

Bake or steam sweet potatoes in their skins until tender, then peel (skin tears off easily after cooking) and mash, adding spices and butter. Lay rows of sliced apples into a buttered 13 x 9 baking dish. Cover with sweet potato mixture and bake at 375° for 30 minutes, or until apples are tender.

Sour Cream Vegetable Stroganoff

Vegetables can be prepared to fit whatever mood you're in, from simple to elegant. This dish is filling enough to be a family favorite, while dinner-party guests will likely ask for the recipe.

½ green pepper, chopped fine
1 carrot, grated
1 medium zucchini, grated
1 cup minced fresh parsley
1 teaspoon basil
½ teaspoon thyme
¼ teaspoon rosemary
1 bay leaf
2 tablespoon olive oil
⅔ cup each: sliced carrots, zucchini, and cauliflower
½ cup peas
3 cups white sauce
½ to ¾ cup sour cream
cooked noodles

Sauté the green pepper, parsley, and herbs in oil for 5 minutes. Add the grated carrot and zucchini and sauté for 5 minutes more. Add bay leaf. Add sauce, cover and simmer, stirring occasionally, for 1 ½ to 2 hours, until sauce is thick. Steam the sliced carrots, zucchini, cauliflower, and peas until tender. Drain thoroughly. Add sour cream to the sauce, then the veggies. Sprinkle with pepper. Serve over cooked noodles.

Red Cabbage with Apples

1 head red cabbage
2 to 3 apples, cored and sliced
1 teaspoon butter
1 teaspoon flour
¼ cup brown sugar
salt to taste

Mix flour smooth in a little water. Place it and remaining ingredients in sauce pan. Pour 2 cups of boiling water over the mixture and cook for 10 minutes or until tender. Add 1 teaspoon lemon juice.

Scrambled Potatoes

3 medium diced potatoes, lightly steamed
1 small zucchini or yellow squash, diced
½ medium green pepper, chopped
½ pound tofu, cubed
2 fresh tomatoes or 1 (16-ounce) can tomatoes
½ teaspoon ground rosemary
1 teaspoon parsley
¼ teaspoon paprika
¼ teaspoon black pepper

Sauté tofu and spices. Add potatoes and sauté until brown, adding zukes and/or squash about halfway before potatoes are done. Add tomatoes at the end just long enough to warm them.

Fancy Fried Potatoes

2 medium potatoes, sliced
½ yellow squash, sliced
½ green pepper, diced
1 stalk celery, sliced
salt and pepper to taste

Fry in butter or margarine until lightly browned.

Broccoli with Cinnamon

Sprinkle broccoli with cinnamon. (Try it, you'll like it.)

Squashes

Squashes have a mild, pleasant flavor and are easy to prepare. Summer squashes (zuccinni and yellow) cook quickly in their skins. Hardshelled winter squashes can be cut in half, the seeds scooped out with a large spoon (the seeds can be roasted and eaten too), then baked, boiled, steamed, or fried. Serve whole, halved or mashed, with butter, honey or brown sugar, or mixed into other dishes.

- **Acorn** (round, green, ribbed): Bake on cookie sheet at 400° for 30 to 40 minutes. If halved, add a teaspoon of brown sugar and a dab of butter before baking.
- **Banana** (large, long, cylindrical, pointed at both ends): Bake at 400° for 30 to 40 minutes. Good in pies too.
- **Butternut** (brown or dark yellow squash, gourd shaped, round bottom, narrow top): Can be boiled, baked, made into soup or pan-fried. Peel for boiling, and slice, boil in salted water for about ten minutes, and mash, add nutmeg and butter. Cut lower portions in quarters for baking, bake at 375° for 45 minutes in a covered pan with water in the bottom of the pan.
- **Hubbard** (large, ridged, spherical squash tapered at both ends): Cut in serving-size pieces, dot with butter, bake 45 to 60 minutes in 375° oven. Great with maple syrup and toasted pecans. Also good for pies.
- **Spaghetti** Squash (medium, yellow skinned, long oval shape): This squash, with its stingy, spaghetti-like meat, is a lot of fun. Cut in half and bake or boil until tender.

- **Yellow** and **Zucchini**: (soft, cylindrical-shaped): While many other squashes are hard-shelled and require long cooking, yellow and zucchini squashes need to be cooked only a few minutes.
- **Zucchini** (a poetic name for the dark green, cylindrical summer squash) is one of the most versatile of all vegetables. Besides familiar uses it can be used as a dessert, pickled, made into jams, and even into ice cream. I suggest you read *The Best of the Zucchini Recipes Cookbook*, Sterling Cookbooks, P.O. Box 16, Pendel, PA 19047.)

Quick Cheddar Squash Casserole

1 small zucchini sliced
1 yellow squash, sliced
1 ½ cups dried bread, lightly toasted
½ cup grated cheddar cheese
1 egg or substitute
1-2 cups milk
Parmesan cheese
Bread crumbs
Butter

Toss the squash, bread and cheddar cheese together in a large, lightly greased baking dish. Beat egg or egg substitute and milk together and pour over squash mixture. Sprinkle Parmesan cheese and bread crumbs on top and dot with butter. Bake 30 minutes at 350°.

Eggplant and Zucchini Mix

1 medium eggplant, diced
3 ribs celery, sliced
1 medium zucchini, diced
1 teaspoon basil
1 teaspoon coriander
½ cup olive oil
1 can tomatoes, sliced into quarters

Heat ½ cup olive oil in skillet over medium heat. Add remaining ingredients. When almost tender, add tomatoes. Serve over steamed rice.

Zucchini

Here are a couple of the great recipes from the *Best of the Zucchini Recipes Cookbook.*

Mock Crab Cakes

2 cups grated zucchini, squeezed as dry as possible
1 cup seasoned bread crumbs
2 tablespoons mayonnaise
2 eggs or substitutes
2 teaspoons Old Bay Seasoning
½ teaspoon salt
1 teaspoon chopped celery

Combine ingredients, mix, and shape into cakes. Fry, browning each side.

Zucchini Fritters

1 cup flour
½ cup milk
1 teaspoon baking powder
1 teaspoons salt
1 teaspoon melted butter
2 beaten eggs or egg substitute
3 teaspoons sugar
1 teaspoon vanilla
3 cups grated zucchini, squeezed dry

Mix all ingredients, except zucchini. Add zucchini. Drop by tablespoonfuls into hot oil. Fry, browning both sides. Drain on paper towels. Sprinkle with powdered sugar.

Zu Sauce

This tastes like applesauce.

4 cups zucchini purée
3 teaspoons lemon juice
½ cup sugar
Optional: 2 drops red food coloring
dash cinnamon

Peel, seed and chop zucchini coarsely. Cook with lemon juice until tender, stirring to prevent burning. If zucchini is dry, add water. Blend until smooth, return blended squash to saucepan with rest of ingredients, cooking and stirring until mixture reaches desired consistency.

CHAPTER 15
Breakfast

"Who would have thought there were so many choices?"

As a new vegetarian three decades ago, feeling sorry for myself because I didn't know any other options, I lamented, "If I don't eat eggs, bacon, sausage, steak, pork chops, pizza, or sugar-coated breakfast cereals, what is left to eat for breakfast?" I laugh now because I learned, from years of thinking outside the cereal box that vegetarian breakfast is another instance where what seems like a loss turns out to be a gain. What's there to eat for vegetarian breakfast? The answer is, a feast!

> **Rule of Tongue for Breakfast**: ***Eat light. Have you noticed that eating a farm-hand style breakfast leaves you feeling loggy and dull? That's because digestion isn't fully awake until lunch time.***
>
> ***Note: "light" doesn't mean donuts. High sugar and carbs start the day with nervous energy and mental flightiness.***

"Cold" Cereals

Let's start understanding vegetarian breakfast with something you are already familiar with: cold cereals. Made from grains, found in any grocery or health food store, in boxes or in bulk, with or without added sugar, usually eaten with cold milk, such cereals are quick and easy. But why settle for the same old stuff? Let your imagination go wild; if you don't like what's in the chart below, then dream up some favorite mixtures of your own, such as mixing applesauce with sweetened whipped cream as a topping for cereals.

Toppings for Cereals (hot or cold)

Sweeteners: *raw, brown or turbano sugars; honey, molasses; stevia (an intensely sweet herb) can be purchased in liquid or crystal form.*

Fruits: *fresh, frozen, canned, or in jams and jellies, including blueberries, raspberries, strawberries, pears peaches, nectarines, pineapples, oranges, grapefruit, grapes, plums, bananas*

Dried fruits *such as raisins, dates, figs, apricots, pineapple, cherries, blueberries*

Coconut, *fresh or packaged, grated*

Nuts *such as almonds, walnuts, pecans, filberts*

Trail Mixes and Granola: *these can be homemade to suit your personal taste, or they can be purchased in grocery or health good stores*

Wheat Germ

Spices *such as cinnamon, cardamom, nutmeg, etc.*

Flavorings *such as vanilla, almond, walnut, etc.*

Milk Substitutes for Cereals

Want to eliminate milk from your diet? Try these substitutes.

Milk Substitute for Cereals

Herb Teas
Any kind, served piping hot or at room temperature

Fruit Juices
To make it thicker and more nutritious, blend with a banana.

Pina Colada Breakfast Cocktail milk substitute: *blend 1 cup pina colada juice with ½ banana. Pour over sliced strawberries (or other fruit) and dry cereal*

Coconut Milk
Use canned coconut milk, or make fresh: for each cup of grated fresh coconut meat, add 2 cups hot water. Let soak 30 minutes (or blend in blender) then squeeze through cheese cloth.

Coconut Cream
Same recipe above using one cup water instead of two.

Nut Milks
Nut milks are available at your health food store, or make them yourself. Just blend ⅓ cup blanched, unsalted almonds or cashews with two cups water

Rice, Almond, or Soy Milk
Comes in pre-mixed or in powder form, in plain, vanilla, or other flavors.

Ancient Rules of Tongue for Good Health

- ***Because cold foods dampen digestive "fires," it's better to warm them before eating. This particularly applies to milk. If you don't enjoy hot milk, then at least take the chill off when it's fresh from the refrigerator, before adding to cereal.***
- ***Boiling milk makes it more digestible, as does adding ghee (clarified butter) and/or add a pinch of ginger. Cardamom and cinnamon add flavor.***
- ***To avoid chemicals from pesticides and fertilizers, and to avoid foods that have been genetically tampered, remember to read labels and buy organic.***

Hot Cereals

Hot cereals are hearty, simple, and nutritious. Remember how good Cream of Wheat and Malt-O-Meal tasted when you were a kid? Or, if you were one of those problem children who refused to eat anything not coated in sugar, you may want to see what they taste like now that you are an adult. Try them with various toppings which may not have been available when you were a child (see list below). Chances are, you'll feel like you've made an important taste discovery. Here are some traditional favorites:

Oatmeal	**Oat bran**	**Multi-grain**
Malt-o-Meal	**Ralston**	**Wheat Germ**
Wheatena	**Cream of Rice**	**Corn Grits**
Farina, sold as.....	**Cream of Wheat**	**Kamut**

Cooked millet, rye, Ammarath, rice, corn or any other grain is totally suitable for breakfast. Cornbread works well too. Just add sweetener and butter and other favorite topping.

Oatmeal

Remember oatmeal from your childhood? It's highly nutritious, digestible, and delicious, low in calories and filling.

Oatmeal Tips

- ***Oatmeal is great for dieters because it "sticks to the ribs", very filling so you are less hungry.***
- ***"Old fashioned" oats take longer to cook but taste better than instant.***
- ***To make oatmeal smooth, add the flakes with the water at the start of cooking.***
- ***Adding a pinch of salt enhances the sweetness. You can add more sweet with sugar, maple syrup, honey, raisins, and/or cut-up dates.***
- ***Add butter.***

Golden Apple Granola

4 cups old-fashioned rolled oats
3 cups chopped apples
¾ cup whole wheat flour
½ cup chopped walnuts
¼ cup brown sugar, packed
½ teaspoon cinnamon
¼ teaspoon salt
1 cup apple juice
½ cup dates, chopped
¼ cup oil
1 teaspoon vanilla

Combine oats, apples, flour, walnuts, brown sugar, cinnamon, and salt. Heat apple juice; add dates and let stand 15 minutes or until softened. Mash and blend well; slowly beat in oil and vanilla. Pour mixture over dry ingredients; stir to moisten evenly. Crumble in thin layer on greased large baking sheet. Bake at 350° for 10 minutes. Reduce heat to 250°

and continue baking for one hour. Stir. Bake 1 ½ to 2 hours longer or until mixture is dry. Stir every 45 minutes. Makes 6 to 7 cups. Store in air tight container.

Hot Granola: add 1 cup granola to 1 ½ cup boiling water. Stir and cook three to five minutes.

Fruits

Light, nutritious, and easily digestible, fruit is perfect for breakfast either by itself or as a topping. Even a few slices sprinkled over pancakes or waffles turns an "ordinary" breakfast into a heart- and tummy-warming event. Fresh, frozen, canned; cooked or au natural; heated or at room temperature; mixed in a fruit cocktail, by itself or used as a topping; plain or garnished—no matter how you serve fruit, it's wonderful. An easy trick to keep breakfast interesting is to look in any desert book for tropical delicacies. (Just remember to go easy on the sugar.)

Apples, Almonds, and Yogurt

Apples are easy and always nutritious. Slice them cooked or raw into oatmeal or dry cereal, or cook in a small sauce pan with raisins, sugar, cinnamon and a little water until tender, and wow! They make a totally nutritious treat for eating either as is, or mixed into any hot or cold cereal, or use this recipe.

⅓ cup sliced almonds
24 whole cloves
6 medium sized tart green apples, peeled and cored
⅔ cup sugar
1 cup water
½ cup plain yogurt
Dash of almond extract

Spread almonds in a shallow pan and toast in a 350° oven for about 8 minutes or until lightly browned. While almonds are browning, insert 4 cloves around the top of each apple, then set aside. Combine sugar and water in wide sauce pan and bring to a boil, stirring until sugar dissolves. Set apples in sugar mix. Cover, reduce heat to low; cook, basting apples with syrup several times, until tender (approximately 12 to 15 minutes).

To serve, place each apple in a shallow desert dish. Stir together yogurt with almond extract; spoon into center of each apple. Spoon syrup around apples and sprinkle with almonds. Serve warm or at room temperature.

Bananas Managua

- 3 large, firm, ripe bananas, peeled, sliced diagonally ¼ inch thick
- ⅓ cup orange juice
- 2 tablespoons firmly packed brown sugar
- 1 teaspoon ground cinnamon
- 3 tablespoons lime or lemon juice
- ¾ cup sour cream or tofu sour cream

Option A: Pour juice over sliced bananas in one bowl; mix sugar and cinnamon in another. Melt 1 tablespoon of butter in a 9 inch frying pan over medium heat. Dip banana slices about ⅓ at a time, into orange juice and then into the brown sugar mixture, then cook in butter until lightly browned on both sides, about 1 minute total. When all are cooked, add lime or lemon juice and any remaining orange juice and brown sugar. This will quickly become syrupy; pour this syrup evenly over bananas. Top each serving with sour cream.

Option B: If your time is limited, forget the cooking; just mix and enjoy.

Rice and Berry Breakfast

2 cups rice, cooked
2 cups fresh blueberries, raspberries or blackberries
1 teaspoon grated lemon peel
1 cup plain yogurt
toasted wheat germ or chopped nuts (optional)
cinnamon (optional)

Combine rice, berries, lemon peel and yogurt. Stir gently. If desired, garnish with wheat germ or nuts, or serve sprinkled with cinnamon. You can buy granola already prepared, but the best way to get the precise taste you like is to create it yourself. Experiment until you find that just right combination.

Merry Berry Soup

Fruit soups are great right from the spoon, or as a topping for dry cereals, or a syrup for hot cereals, or to pour like sauce over other fruit or toast.

4 cups tart berries (such as boysenberries, raspberries, or currants) fresh or frozen (thawed)
1 cup water
⅔ cup sugar (omit sugar if using frozen berries packed in syrup)
1 ½ tablespoon cornstarch
2 tablespoons water
Optional: whipping cream, cream, sour cream, or tofu sour cream.

Combine 1 cup water, sugar, and fruit and bring to boil. Cook for 1 or 2 minutes. Blend cornstarch with the 2 tablespoons water and stir into berry mixture. Stirring gently, return to a boil then allow to thicken as it cools. Serve hot or cool. (For a smoother, seedless soup, pour the berry-sugar mixture through a strainer before adding the cornstarch.)

Blueberry Soup

1 pint blueberries
2 cups water
¼ cup honey
1 stick cinnamon
1 lemon, thinly sliced
1 cup plain, fresh yogurt

Simmer blueberries, water, cinnamon and lemon for ten minutes. After mixture cools, strain through a cheesecloth, pressing hard to extract all the juices, add honey and yogurt and stir. (For a thicker soup, during cooking add arrowroot creamed in water.)

Note: If preparation of these yummy pudding and soup recipes take longer than you can manage in the mornings, try making them the night before, then warm briefly before serving to take off the chill.

Breakfast with Breads

Historians don't know which was created first, bread or beer. Breads and grains, often called "the staff of life," are the most ancient and respectable of foods. Bread is made from the same grains found in breakfast cereals—and it is quick and easy. You can make or buy a variety of breads, including raisin breads, bagels, and so forth, perhaps keeping them in the freezer until needed. Forget the white fluff; go for the whole grains.

Our ancestors tore their portions directly from the loaf, probably eating it without garnish or side dishes. In today's world, with so many other options, you may not have given much attention to plain, unadorned breads with their deeply satisfying taste, as breakfast fare. However, breads are quick, nutritious, and there are countless ways of preparing it. As toast it can not only be spread it with butter, ghee, jams, jellies, honey, syrups, but with *anything* you enjoy.

Heaven On Earth Breakfast Sandwich

On toast, spread honey or maple syrup, sprinkle with raisins and nuts. Blueberries and coconut optional. Pour syrup light to eat it like a sandwich, or heavy to enjoy it like French toast.

Nut and Fruit Breads

Nut and fruit breads are easy, delicious, nutritious—and portable. This means that if you are like many of us who haven't yet reached the point in life where we are more concerned with good health than with getting "somewhere," nut- and fruit-breads are quick, filling and nutritious. I know from past experience that they can be eaten in the car or subway on the way to work.

Banana Nut Bread

⅓ cup butter, margarine or shortening
½ cup sugar
2 eggs or substitutes
1 ¾ cups flour
1 teaspoon baking powder
⅓ teaspoon soda
½ teaspoon salt
1 cup ripe banana, mashed
½ cup walnuts, chopped

Cream shortening and sugar, add eggs or substitutes. Beat well. Mix dry ingredients in a separate bowl. Add to creamed mixture alternately with banana, blending well after each addition. Stir in nuts. Pour into well-greased 9x5 loaf pan. Bake 350° 45 to 50 minutes or until done. Remove from pan to cool.

Breakfast Cakes, Cookies, Pies & Puddings

Surprised to see deserts on the list of breakfast options? Consider: most deserts are made of the same ingredients as breakfast cereal, i.e. grains, fruits, nuts, raisins, dates, sweeteners, etc. For improved nutrition, leave out as much of the sweeteners and processed foods as possible, use hearty whole flours and fresh ingredients (preferably organic and free from genetic tampering). Try modifying or using any favorite desert recipe as is for breakfast and see if it doesn't make you look forward to morning.

Choose cakes with less sugar and no icing, such as the **Ranch Apple Cake** recipe on page 135. Add fruit or other toppings such as butter. Example: white or cherry cake, spread with cream cheese or sour cream, heaped with canned cherry pie filling. Heat briefly in the toaster oven.

Cookies

I haven't included cookie recipes because they are easy to find. Oatmeal and raisins or pumpkin make good breakfast cookies. The high sugar, preservative-laden and poor-ingredient store-bought cookies should be avoided.

Pies

Pumpkin pie is great for breakfast, as are cream, nut, and fruit pies. Loaded with taste and nutrition, they are especially good if you make them from 'scratch,' without all the chemicals and artificial stuff found in store-bought.

Breakfast Puddings

You can use packaged organic pudding mixes or make pudding from scratch. Homemade means less sugar and artificial ingredients. Hot cereals also make great pudding base, like this one following.

Farina Pudding with Fruit Sauce

⅔ cup farina
1 quart milk or milk substitute
½ teaspoon vanilla
⅜ cup sugar
2 eggs, separated (or egg substitute)
Cherry or Raspberry Sauce (see below)

Bring the milk to a boil, gradually add farina, stirring continuously to avoid lumps. Add sugar and vanilla and cook until thick. Beat egg whites (or egg substitute) until stiff, then add to cooled cream of wheat mixture. Pour into a buttered two-quart mold. Serve with raspberry sauce below.

Sauces for Cooked Cereals, Puddings and Breads (Pancakes or Toast)

Syrups, sweeteners and sauces turn make hot cereals from kiddie-mush into dramatic dining. Following are two examples of fruit sauces that work for **Farina Pudding**, or any other favorite breakfast recipe, or creates an exciting dressings for toast or pancakes. To make your own special fruit sauce, use fresh, canned or frozen fruit, mix it with a bit of water and (organic!) corn syrup or sugar or whatever sweetener you prefer. Cook over low heat until smooth.

Ayurvedic Rule of Tongue

Don't cook with honey as heating changes its structure so that it doesn't digest well. Add honey only after cooking.

Cherry Sauce

2 cups ripe, fresh cherries, pitted, or 2 cup canned cherries, drained
¼ cup water or cherry juice
1 tablespoon sugar

¼ cup orange juice
1 tablespoon water
1 tablespoon cornstarch
1 tablespoon butter

Bring cherries, water or juice, sugar, and orange juice to a boil. Thicken with cornstarch. Add butter, mix well. Pour over pudding.

Raspberry Sauce

1 cup raspberry syrup
1 cup water
½ teaspoon lemon juice

Combine ingredients and bring to a boil. Add a little cornstarch if you prefer a thicker sauce. Stir well and serve over the pudding.

Date Rice Pudding

1 cup rice, cooked
½ cup chopped dates
⅓ cup milk or milk substitute
¼ cup maple syrup
1 egg, separated, or egg substitute
1 teaspoon vanilla
1 tablespoon sugar

To rice, add all ingredients except egg whites and sugar. Cook over boiling water for 5 to 6 minutes or until thickened, stirring frequently. Beat egg white (or substitute) with sugar until stiff and fold into pudding. Serve warm or cool.

Tapioca Fruit Pudding

2 cups berry juice
⅓ cup honey
1 teaspoons vanilla extract
¼ cup tapioca flour or arrowroot

Mix juice, vanilla and tapioca or arrowroot in a small saucepan. Bring to a boil, then turn down heat and simmer for five minutes or until slightly thickened, stirring frequently. Remove from heat. Add honey and mix well. Pour into individual glass dishes and allow to cool. To add visual and taste delight, garnish with yogurt, whole berries, and edible blossoms, such as violets, nasturtiums, borage flowers , rose petals, or marigolds.

Substitutes for Eggs, Meats and Gravies

Spiced right, soft tofu makes a very credible substitute for scrambled eggs and meats. You might want to use margarine rather than butter in the following dishes because it has an "eggier" taste than butter, ghee or other oils.

Scrambled Egg-fu

1 pound fresh tofu, drained
½ teaspoon thyme
¼ teaspoon celery seed
⅛ teaspoon turmeric
½ cup milk
salt and pepper to taste
margarine to coat skillet

Heat margarine in skillet. Beat ingredients to smooth consistency and pour into heated skillet. Cook until it has the consistency of scrambled eggs. Optional: add chopped celery and/or bok choy, green peppers, and tomatoes.

Tomato and Basil "Omelet"

6 eggs or 1 pound fresh, soft tofu
8-10 basil leaves, minced
1 large tomato, sliced
1 tablespoon olive oil
2 tablespoons grated Parmesan or Gruyere cheese
basil leaves for garnish.

Mix eggs or tofu and basil. Remove seeds from the tomato slices and blot slices as dry as possible. Pour egg (tofu) mixture and cook over medium high heat, gently lifting the sides of the omelet to let uncooked eggs (tofu) flow underneath. Cook four to five minutes until edges have set and eggs (tofu) are golden on bottom. Top will not be entirely set.

Remove pan from heat and place tomato slices on top of omelet. Sprinkle with cheese. Place pan six inches from broiler. Broil until top is golden and puffed (2-3 minutes). Garnish with basil leaves.

Granolas and Trail Mixes

Home Made Granola

10 cups "old-fashioned" oats
3 cups wheat germ
1 cup brown sugar
2 cups hot water
1 cup oil

Mix oats and wheat germ,. In another container, blend brown sugar, water and oil. Add to oats mixture. Mix well. Spread mixture on cookie sheet in a thin layer. Bake at 325° for about 30 minutes, stirring occasionally. (Edges will brown too quickly if not stirred.) Let cool. Store in an air-tight container. Keeps 1 ½ months.

You can personalize home-made or store-bought granola or trail mixes by adding:

- sesame or sunflower seeds
- nuts
- raisins, plain or covered with yogurt
- dried blueberries, or other dried fruits
- shredded coconut

Because they burn easily, wait until after baking before adding raisins or dried fruits

Other breakfast ideas:

- Homemade whole-wheat donuts
- Nut Rolls
- Warmed melba toast
- Popovers
- Cornmeal, buckwheat, griddle cakes
- Corn fritters
- Cornmeal mush
- Crepes or blintz pancakes
- Fruit dumplings served with:
  - Butter
  - Syrup or honey
  - Gravy
  - Milk or yogurt
  - Fresh fruit
  - Jellies and jams
- Bagels, alone or with creame cheese or other dressing
- Croutons, served with butter, honey, gravy, or milk, and/or tossed with fresh fruit

If you really miss the taste of bacon and sausage, good taste-a-likes are available in the deli or freezer section of the grocery store. (Don't forget to read the labels.)

CHAPTER 16
Sandwiches

"Why, I like this even better than meat!"

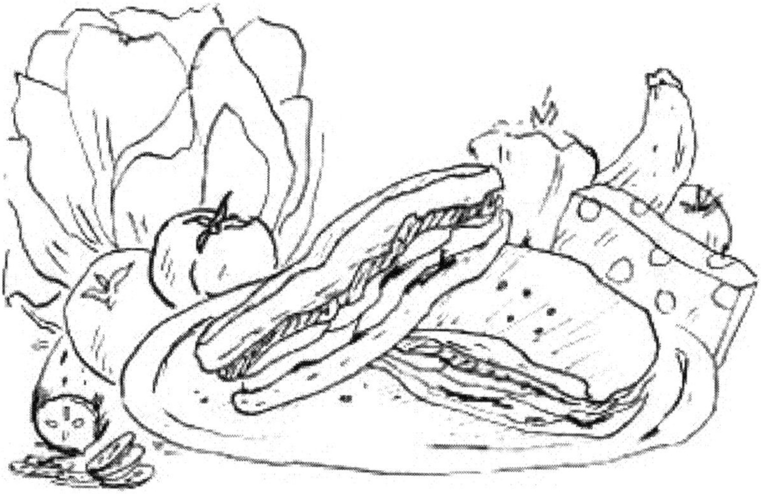

Does the individual who decides to stop eating meat have to give up sandwiches? Absolutely not! We simply switch from meat thinking to all-possibilities thinking. It is said that the 4th Earl of Sandwich got the idea of wrapping meat in bread to keep his playing cards free of grease. Isn't it equally practical to protect your playing cards from the oils in your avocado?

So when you think, *sandwich,* don't get stuck thinking of ham slices or meat burgers. Instead, think of any favorite food, then think what tastes you like with it. Put it all together between two pieces of any style of bread or crackers, and presto: you have a new favorite sandwich. Here's the rule for sandwiches: anything goes. If it's edible it can go into a sandwich.

Create A Sandwich With:

- **Anything you'd use in a salad:** lettuce, tomatoes, chopped or sliced green peppers, sliced or mashed and spiced avocado, shredded carrots, chopped celery, sliced or shredded olives, chopped or sliced or leaf bok choy (tastes like onions), sliced cucumbers, sprouts, water chestnuts.
- **Anything sweet and gooey:** jelly, jam, honey, nutbutters, creamery butter, ghee, whole or mashed bananas, apple sauce, apple or other fruit butters etc.
- **Any cooked vegetable (mashed, sliced, or shredded):** potatoes (white or sweet), eggplant, asparagus, broccoli, cauliflower etc.
- **Any bean:** pureed beans, tempe, or any style tofu (plain or spiced) etc.
- **Any fruit, nut, or seed:** (cooked or raw) raisins, apples, bananas, kiwi fruit, pineapple, avocado, cranberry, sesame seeds, sunny seeds etc.
- **Any sauce, gravy, or salad dressing** can be used on open-faced sandwiches, or as a substitute for mayonnaise, mustard, ketchup etc.

Cheese Sandwiches

Lets begin our sandwich adventure from a place we are already comfortably familiar—cheese sandwiches. Then we'll expand to new territory. The only rule is, no matter how strange the recipes sound, try them. Repeated experience provides opportunities to develop new tastes, and chances are you'll end up loving a lot of new favorites.

Classic Grilled Cheese Sandwich

Butter two slices of bread, place the cheese between with the butter outside. Brown on each side in heavy skillet or griddle.

Variations:

- add avocado and/or tomato and/or black olives
- experiment with different types of cheese
- try broiling instead of frying
- try frying with olive oil rather than butter.

The surest way to find a sandwich you really like is: experiment.

Grilled Olive-Cheese Sandwiches

12 slices bread
1 cup grated cheese
¼ cup chopped ripe or green olives
2 tablespoons chopped pimento
1 teaspoon dry mustard or 2 teaspoons prepared mustard
1 stick butter, softened, for buttering bread

Combine first four ingredients. Butter six slices of bread, then spread with the cheese mixture. Cover with remaining slices. Cook in skillet until crisp and golden brown on both sides.

Cheese Spread Mix

Mix 1 ½ cups of shredded cheddar with 1 teaspoon pickle relish or chutney and ½ cup mayonnaise.

Vegetarian Hero Sandwich

For a quick feast, slice Italian or French bread lengthwise. Spread with butter and/or mayonnaise and/or mustard. Build sandwich with overlapping slices of Cheddar, Swiss, fontina, and provolone or other favorite cheeses. Add lettuce, sliced tomatoes, strips of sweet peppers, sliced or chopped olives ... yumm. Add herbs if you like, then eat as is or toast first.

Bread and Cheese and Apples

Partaking of this combination makes you a part of history, connecting you to countless souls who have eaten these foods from hillsides overlooking flocks of sheep, sitting at rough-hewn tables, rocking on the backs of camels and horses, leaning against a tree at romantic picnics, or eating them combined in gourmet dishes at classy restaurants.

To make, simply layer sliced cheese and thin-sliced apples between slices of your favorite bread. Mayonnaise, not available in ancient times, is optional.

Cheese, Carrots, and Raisin Sandwich

cheese, sliced
1 carrot, grated
1 tablespoon chopped raisins
lettuce

Places cheese slices on whole wheat or other bread. Sprinkle with carrots and raisins. Top with lettuce, mayonnaise and second bread slice.

Cream Cheese

Basic Cream Cheese Sandwich

Cream cheese makes an ideal sandwich base. It compliments the flavor of many favorite tastes.

1 8-ounce package cream cheese
1 to 3 tablespoons yogurt, cream, or olive oil

Whip the cream cheese until smooth, adding the yogurt, cream, or olive oil as needed if it is too thick. Spread on bread.

Cream Cheese Options:

Try one or a combination of the following suggestions for quick, easy and creative sandwiches using cream cheese:

- Add fresh chopped or dried herbs such as mint, basil, tarragon, fennel; or spices such as cinnamon, coriander, or black pepper. Add zing with a sprinkle of lemon juice.
- Beat in a little tomato paste for color.
- Add cucumber, grated and pressed dry with a paper towel.
- Add celery, chopped fine, with sliced olives.
- Add chopped walnuts (sugar optional).
- Spread on cinnamon raisin bread and toast lightly in oven.
- Consult the cottage cheese section (following) for ideas such as adding sliced or chopped black olives, chopped and drained pineapple.

Cottage Cheese Sandwiches

Cottage cheese on a sandwich? Yep, it's delicious

Cottage Cheese and Yogurt Sandwich

Blend equal quantities of cottage cheese and yogurt. Add fixings, or use as a spread in place of mayonnaise. Add lettuce or sprouts and tomato, or any favorite toppings.

Pepper Pineapple Cottage Cheese Sandwich

1 cup cottage cheese
3 tablespoons each:
  olives, sliced or chopped
  pineapple, drained and chopped
  sweet peppers, chopped
1 tablespoon parsley, chopped

Mix ingredients; add salt and pepper to taste. Spread on bread.

Cottage Cheese and Bananas

1 banana
½ cup cottage cheese

Mash banana and combine with cottage cheeses. For a special taste treat, serve on cinnamon raisin whole wheat bread.

Other cottage cheese ideas:

- Toast sandwich in skillet or toaster oven.
- Use as a spread (like mayonnaise) for other sandwich recipes.
- Add any salad fixin's for toppings.
- Cream cheese ideas (above) work for cottage cheese too.

Nutbutter Sandwiches

Nutbutters such as cashew or almond are hearty and can be used alone or with a variety of fruits and vegetables, on plain bread or toast. (According to Ayurveda, peanut butter clogs the body channels but if you choose, it can also used in any nutbutter recipe.)

Start with these basic combinations, then experiment with chopped nuts, shredded coconut, other sliced fruits, jams and jellies, honey, and other flavors and toppings.

Apple Cashew Butter Sandwich

Spread bread with cashew butter, then cover with sliced apples and second piece of bread. Awesome.

Banana Cashew Butter Sandwich

Spread bread with cashew butter, then layer with banana slices and cover with second slice of bread.

Nutbutter Sandwich Spread

½ cup chickpeas, cooked and pureed
¼ cup cashew butter
¼ cup almond butter
¼ teaspoon mustard seed
¼ teaspoon cumin
¼ teaspoon coriander
¼ teaspoon caraway

Blend ingredients thoroughly and spread on bread or crackers.

Vegetable Sandwich Spreads

Wonderful sandwich spreads can be made out of almost anything edible. Add any favorite cooked vegetable (sliced or mashed) onto a slice of bread, cover with any favorite soup, cheese sauce, white sauce (page 212) or gravy. Got unexpected guests? Add a sprig of parsley, cooked fresh peas, and/or some strips of red and green sweet pepper. In a moment's notice, you can turn the simple into gourmet and get rave reviews.

Green Cauliflower Sandwich Spread

1 cup cauliflower, cooked
3 cups (yes, cups) fresh basil leaves
salt and pepper to taste if desired

Purêe cauliflower and basil leaves in blender with a little water until a smooth paste is formed. Use as a sandwich spread by itself or garnish with tomatoes, avocado slices, lettuce, or other favorites. Optional: for a thicker spread, add ½ cup chick-peas, cooked and pureed.

Guacamole/Avocado Cream Sandwich

2 large avocados, mashed
a few drops olive oil
salt and pepper to taste, if desired
pinch of sugar
juice of ½ to 1 whole lime or lemon
½ cup green pepper, finely chopped
1 tomato, peeled, seeded, and chopped
½ cup fresh coriander leaves, chopped fine

Blend avocados, olive oil, and spices until smooth. Mix in remaining ingredients and spread over bread. For variety, add a layer of salsa.

Mashed Potato Sandwiches

Spread mashed potatoes on buttered bread, adding seasonings and other vegetables (such as cooked corn) as desired.

Open-Faced Sandwiches

Open-face Asparagus Sandwiches

6 stalks asparagus, cooked until tender
1 tablespoon butter
1 tablespoon flour
⅓ cup asparagus liquid
¼ cup milk or substitute
salt and pepper, if desired
¼ cup grated Parmesan
¼ cup Provolone, shredded
4 slices white or rye toast

Simmer butter, flour, asparagus liquid and milk until smooth. Add salt and pepper to taste. Stir in cheeses, cooking until cheese is melted. Lay asparagus spears on toast and cover with hot cheese sauce. Place under broiler until sauce is lightly browned.

Other ideas for open-faced sandwiches:

- Place cooked spinach on toast then cover with Swiss cheese sauce (add shredded cheese to a white sauce and heat until melted).
- Pour cream or dark gravy over tofu beefsteak (page 79) and mashed potatoes layered over bread or biscuits; season with herbs and spices.

Eggplant Sandwiches

Eggplant, called "the poor man's caviar" in the Middle East, is used world wide as a substitute for meat. It makes a delicious and hearty sandwich filling—or even a replacement for the bread. To take out any bitterness, sprinkle the eggplant with salt and let stand for 30 minutes. Rinse and wipe dry before cooking. Heat oil first to prevent excess absorption.

Eggplant Purêe Sandwich Spread

1 eggplant, sliced
1 tablespoon olive oil
juice of 1 lemon
salt and pepper
parsley
fresh mint leaves
fresh basil leaves

Sauté eggplant in olive oil until its skin turns black and blisters. Peel off skins, squeeze out excess juices, mash with a fork or puree in a blender. Add remaining ingredients and mix well. Spread on bread.

For variety, add yogurt, peeled and chopped or sliced tomatoes, chopped black olives, cooked sliced zucchini ... or anything else that's edible.

Eggplant Sandwich, sans Bread

1 medium eggplant, peeled and sliced in ½ inch widths
1 teaspoon basil
½ teaspoon thyme
½ teaspoon oregano
1 cup bread crumbs

½ cup mozzarella cheese, powdered or shredded
2 eggs or egg substitutes, mixed with 3 tablespoons water or milk
olive oil for frying
salt and pepper to taste

On a sheet of waxed paper, mix breadcrumbs and herbs. Dip each sandwich in beaten egg mixture, then in breadcrumb mixture, until well coated on both sides. Cook in olive oil over medium-high heat 6 to 8 minutes, or until golden brown on both sides. Place on bread and sprinkle with mozzarella cheese, garnish with briefly cooked tomatoes, zucchini, and black olives.

To use eggplant as a replacement for the bread, use above recipe and add a layer of cheese between two patties of eggplant and heat until tender and the cheese melts. Before cooking, top with sliced tomato and olives.

Alternative to frying: Eggplant absorbs oil readily, so you may prefer to bake it: sprinkle with olive oil, bake at 400° about 15 minutes, or until tender.

Optional: cover with tomato sauce before baking.

Bean Spreads

Take any plain or seasoned cooked bean, purêe it to a spreadable consistency, and knife it onto any style bread—white or whole wheat, French or Italian, or corn or flour tortillas, or pocket bread. Spice with your favorite spice or herb. It can then be garnished with as many different toppings as you have the imagination to dream up. *Laurel's Kitchen*, recommends garnishing with cucumber and tomato slices. Another idea is to thin bean purêes with vegetable stock to make a dip for crackers.

Delhi Chickpea Spread Sandwich

Chickpeas—garbanzo beans—make an excellent base for bean spreads or for stuffing pocket bread. Here are a few of innumerable great ideas.

1 cup chickpeas, cooked and purêed
1 green peppers, minced
2 tablespoons vegetable oil
1 tomatoes, peeled, seeded, and chopped
1 ½ teaspoons coriander
1 teaspoon cumin
⅓ teaspoon turmeric
1 ½ tablespoons lemon juice
2 teaspoons garam masala or curry powder
1 ½ teaspoons salt
1 tablespoon fresh ginger root, grated

Mix ingredients well and spread on bread or use in pocket bread. Garnish with lettuce, tomato, and tahini.

Another Style Garbanzo Spread

3 cups garbanzo beans, mashed
juice of one lemon
1 teaspoon basil
½ bunch parsley
½ teaspoon oregano
1 tablespoon oil
salt and pepper to taste if desired
⅔ cup sesame seeds, toasted and ground (optional)

Sauté cumin in oil, add herbs and parsley and cook briefly to soften parsley, then mix with lemon and mashed beans. Add sesame seeds if desired.

Split Pea Sandwich Spread

1 cup green split peas
1 tablespoon oil
2 tablespoons Parmesan cheese
2 tablespoons cottage cheese
¼ teaspoon basil
salt and pepper to taste if desired

Cook peas down into a thick paste (it will get thicker as it cools), and mix well with other ingredients

Kidney Bean Purêe Sandwich Spread

1 cup dry kidney beans, cooked until tender
1 carrot, sliced
1 small green pepper or 2 ribs bok choy, chopped
¼ teaspoon nutmeg
3 teaspoons butter (optional)
salt and pepper to taste

Cook carrot and pepper or bok choy with beans and bay leaf. When the beans are tender, discard the bay leaf, drain off the water, add seasonings and purêe until smooth. Spread on flour bread or hot wedges of cornbread.

Other possibilities for Kidney Bean Spread: use different seasonings, such as parsley, coriander, or savory. Garnish with fresh parsley, shredded cabbage, or tomatoes.

Bean Polenta Creole Sandwich Spread

1 cup navy beans, cooked until tender and drained
½ tablespoon molasses
1 teaspoon prepared mustard
1 teaspoon butter
1 ½ tablespoons lemon juice
salt and pepper to taste

Mix ingredients and puree until smooth. Spread on bread or crackers.

Refried Bean Sandwich

Mash cooked pinto, kidney, or black beans, add Mexican spices such as oregano, cumin or chili powder to taste. Garnish with slices of tomato, green pepper, avocado, black olives, lettuce, sour cream, salsa, or other favorites.

Italian Soy-Veggie or Tofu Sandwich

Mash cooked soybeans or tofu, and add chopped celery, green peppers, and spaghetti sauce to taste. Garnish with sliced black olives and chopped fresh basil.

Pita (Pocket Bread) Sandwiches

Many cultures use thin, flat breads such as corn or flour tortillas to enhance the flavor of foods and to provide a convenient method of holding or traveling with the contents—not only tasty but smart. Pita bread, often called pocket bread, is a round patty of bread which, when sliced in half, opens up inside to create a pocket. Filling up the interiors of these sandwiches is fun, practical, delicious, and infinitely versatile. Stuff with a bean (or other favorite) base, then add your favorite toppings. Try these traditional recipes, then see how many variations you can create on your own.

Pita Bread Fillings

Pick and choose among the following ingredients, experimenting until you find what combinations you most enjoy:

- falafel balls
- sliced tofu
- whole or mashed beans
- tahini
- hummus
- tomatoes, chopped or sliced
- black olives, whole, chopped or sliced
- lettuce
- cucumbers, sliced

More Ideas for Pita Bread Fillings

- **Cream Cheese:** Whip well, adding yogurt, cottage cheese, cream, or olive oil. Flavor with herbs such as mint, basil, and tarragon.
- **Indian Cauliflower filling:** Cook cauliflower and peas separately until tender, then mash. Add cumin, coriander or graham masala, or other favorite Indian spices.
- **Eggplant:** Fry thin eggplant and/or zucchini slices in olive oil. Add tomatoes, black olives, fresh basil. Optional: small slices of cheese. Sprinkle with black pepper and a touch of grated nutmeg.
- **Pizza Pita:** Press into pouch any favorite combination of tomatoes, mozzarella , olives, green peppers, pineapple, pizza sauces, or other pizza toppings.
- **Mexican Pita:** Add Mexican-spiced falafel balls or lentils, lettuce, tomatoes, green peppers, and salsa.
- **Indian mashed potato filling:** Fry half a chopped green pepper in butter and mix with 2 boiled mashed potatoes. Add a few chopped coriander leaves or parsley, a good squeeze of lemon juice, ¼ teaspoon paprika, a pinch of ginger, 1 teaspoon crushed coriander, fennel

or anise, and ½ teaspoon graham masala plus salt and pepper if desired.

- **Hummus fillings:** Use any bean or lentil, cook until very soft, puree; add cooking water to make a thick cream, then add olive oil, lemon juice, pepper, cumin, coriander, pepper, parsley or coriander to taste.

Falafel (Fried Chickpea) Balls for Pita Bread

2 ½ cups dried chickpeas (garbanzo beans), soaked overnight, drained
1 teaspoon ground coriander seeds
1 teaspoon ground cumin
1 teaspoon lemon juice
¼ teaspoon turmeric
salt and pepper to taste, if desired
¼ cup oil

Grind the chickpeas fine in a blender or food processor, and mix them with the spices. Add flour and mix thoroughly. Form small balls (about 1 ½ inches in diameter. Fry the balls, a few at a time, for 2 or 3 minutes, or until golden brown. Serve with pocket bread and garnishes. Traditionally served with tahini.

Tahini is a traditional Middle Eastern topping for pita bread, but it also makes a great spread for other sandwiches.

1 cup sesame butter
⅔ cup lemon juice
½ cup butter
salt and pepper to taste

Mix ingredients and blend until smooth.

Quick method: Falafel mixes and prepared Tahini are available in grocery and health food stores.

Walnut Oatmeal Burgers

1 cup walnuts, ground in blender
1 cup rolled oats, "old fashioned" type
1 egg or egg substitute
¼ cup milk or water
1 stalk bok choy or green pepper, chopped fine
½ teaspoon sage
½ teaspoon salt if desired
salt and pepper to taste

Mix ingredients well. Form into patties. Brown patties in oiled skillet over medium heat. Serve like hamburgers with lettuce, tomato, and your favorite toppings, relishes and sauces.

For moist Walnut Oatmeal Burgers: After burgers are browned, add 1 ½ cups vegetable stock. Bring to a boil, then reduce heat and simmer, covered, for about 25 minutes.

Vegetable Cutlets

2 tablespoons vegetable oil
1 cup chopped green peppers
1 cup carrots, shredded
½ cup celery, chopped
½ cup green beans cut into 1-inch pieces
½ cup peas, fresh or frozen
2 cups bread crumbs, soft
⅓ cup sunflower seeds
½ teaspoon salt
¼ teaspoon basil
¼ teaspoon thyme
⅛ teaspoon pepper
2 eggs or substitute
2 tablespoons wheat germ, toasted
½ cup water
spaghetti sauce

Mix all ingredients except for breadcrumbs, wheat germ, and water. Cook until tender. When done, let cool slightly and stir in bread crumbs and water. Using ½ cup vegetable mixture at a time, shape into 3-inch round cutlets, about ½ inch thick. In 12-inch skillet heat 2 tablespoons oil over medium heat until hot. Cook cutlets, turning once, 6 to 9 minutes or until golden brown on both sides. Serve on bread, spread with a thick layer of heated spaghetti sauce.

Tofu Sandwiches

Tofu is as versatile as your imagination. It can be purêed by itself or with other beans, vegetables, and seasonings, or slices served hot or cold right out of the box the same way you would use a slice of lunch meat, perhaps sprinkled with salt, your favorite salad spice mix, lemon-pepper, barbeque sauce, or other seasonings. Add your favorite sandwich toppings such as condiments, lettuce and tomatoes.

Tofu "Meat" Sandwiches

See the Tofu Hamburger chapter (page 71) for sandwich ideas like tofu beefsteak, sloppy joes, chicken, egg-fu, and others. You can use any tofu "meat" substitute recipe on any sandwich.

More Ideas

Many dry or frozen packaged vegetarian foods now look and taste like meats—burgers, sausages, TVP, and so forth, in the grocery store or market. Just be sure to read labels to make sure ingredients are healthy. Beware of MSG, monosodium glutamate, which is found under the name autolyzed yeast, glutamate, monopotassium glutamate, textured protein, yeast nutrient, yeast extract or yeast food, calcium caseinate, glutamic acid, gelatin, hydrolyzed protein, sodium caseinate.

CHAPTER 17
Soup de Jour

"Ah, the romance of soup."

Soup was one of the first foods created, over 6,000 years ago, and we've never gotten tired of it, not even when they put it in cans with a lot of artificial ingredients. It's still good for the body, good for the soul.

However, in my pre-vegetarian days I assumed non-meat soups would be bland and uninteresting. I had no idea how wonderful soups could be until I began to eat them using all fresh ingredients.

Rule of Tongue for Extra Nutrition

Rather than throw away the nutrition-filled water used to boil or steam vegetables, pour it into a cup and drink it or freeze it for your next soup or stock.

Soups are good any time but they are especially nice for evening meals when we don't want to load up our tummies before bed. Eat them with bread (homemade is especially nice), crackers, pretzels or rice cakes.

My Tomato Vegetable Soup

3 medium potatoes, cubed
3 medium carrots, sliced or cubed
1 green pepper, cubed
1 small zucchini, cubed
2 (16-ounce) cans tomatoes
½ teaspoon marjoram
1 teaspoon vegetable-based chicken flavoring or poultry seasoning
1 teaspoon salt
¼ teaspoon pepper
Water to cover well

Quarter tomatoes. Place vegetables, water, and seasonings in large saucepan. Simmer until veggies are tender. Serve with piping hot cornbread.

My Tomato Vegetable Soup with tofu: Instead of putting the above seasonings directly into the soup, mix them into ½ cup flour. Cut ½ pound tofu into small cubes. Roll tofu in water and then in the flour mixture. Sauté in butter or margarine until lightly browned. Add to cooked soup.

Cream of Spinach Soup

1 10-ounce package frozen spinach, or use fresh spinach, chopped
1 cup water
½ teaspoon salt
¼ teaspoon nutmeg
2 tablespoons butter or ghee
2 tablespoons flour
3 cups milk or substitute

Place spinach, water, salt, and nutmeg in a saucepan. Cover and cook until very tender, then purée. Melt butter in a small saucepan; stir in flour, cook until thick and bubbling. Remove from heat and stir in milk or milk substitute; return to heat and cook until thickened. Add spinach mixture.

Cream of Celery Soup

1 bunch celery, chopped fine
1 quart water
1 teaspoon salt
¼ teaspoon nutmeg
¼ teaspoon celery seed
¼ teaspoon cayenne pepper
2 tablespoons butter
2 tablespoons flour
2 cups milk or milk substitute

Place celery, seasonings, and water in saucepan. Bring to boil, then reduce heat and simmer until celery is tender. Melt butter; stir in flour and then milk or milk substitute. Cook until thickened, stirring constantly. Stir this into the celery mixture and simmer for 5 minutes, stirring until smooth.

Cream of Tomato Soup

1 (16-ounce) can tomatoes in natural juice
1 sprig parsley
1 bay leaf
1 teaspoon salt
1 teaspoon Worcestershire sauce or soy sauce
4 cups water
3 tablespoon butter
2 tablespoons flour

Place tomatoes, seasonings, and water in a saucepan. Cook for 20 minutes, then purée. Melt butter in a small saucepan; add flour and stir until smooth. Pour some of the tomato soup into the butter-flour mixture and stir until very smooth, then gradually return this mixture to the tomato soup, stirring constantly for 3-5 minutes or until thickened.

Coconut Curry Vegetable Soup

1 tablespoon coriander
½ tablespoon cumin seed
½ tablespoon black peppercorns
½ teaspoon whole caraway seed
½ teaspoon fenugreek
½ teaspoon anise seed
1 teaspoon turmeric
½ teaspoon whole cloves
3 cardamom pods
Pinch each, nutmeg, cinnamon and mace
⅓ cup ghee
1 medium green peppers
2 inch piece ginger, peeled and minced
2 tablespoons flour
2 medium white potatoes, diced
1 large carrots, sliced
3 cups vegetable stock (recipe below)

2 cups coconut milk (canned, unsweetened)
1 summer squash, diced
3 tomatoes, diced
1 bunch spinach, cleaned and cut into 2 inch pieces
½ cup cilantro, rough chop
salt and pepper to taste

Grind all the spices and toast them over low heat. Melt the ghee in a large pot. Sauté the green peppers and ginger in the ghee over high heat for 1 to 2 minutes. Reduce heat. Add the flour and cook until the green peppers are soft. Add the potatoes and carrots and sauté for 1 to 2 minutes. Add the stock and cook over high heat until potatoes and carrots are almost done, about 7 to 10 minutes, stirring often. Add the coconut milk and squash, reduce heat, and cook until all the vegetables are tender. Just before serving, add the diced tomatoes, chopped spinach, and cilantro.

Basic Vegetable Stock

3 celery ribs
2 carrots
2 whole tomatoes
2 zucchini or summer squash
1 corncob, if available
1 potato
1 bell pepper, any color
¼ pound string beans
1 bunches parsley
2 bay leaves
Small handful black peppercorns
1 gallon water

Rough chop all the vegetables. Place all ingredients in a large stockpot, bring to a boil, and skim any foam off the surface. Reduce heat and simmer, uncovered, for 3 to 4 hours. Be sure to stir the stock once in a while. Strain and cool before refrigerating. The stock can be reduced to intensify the flavors. Stock will keep for 1 week in the refrigerator, longer in the freezer.

Green Goddess Soup

This is such a pretty soup, and if anything, it is even more delicious than it looks.

2 medium potatoes
1 box frozen spinach, thawed and well drained
1 cup milk
1 tablespoon butter
½ teaspoon nutmeg
2 tablespoons chopped fresh parsley or 1 teaspoon
dried parsley
salt and pepper to taste

Steam potatoes until tender, then mash. Add milk and butter and simmer, stirring until thick and smooth. No more than twenty minutes before serving, add spinach, parsley, and spices. When spinach is limp, purée into a smooth soup. Be careful not to overcook. The soup should turn out a beautiful bright green.

Cheddar Chowder

3 cups water
4 chicken bouillon cubes or 1 teaspoon chicken-
flavor vegetable powder
4 medium potatoes, peeled and diced
1 cup carrots, sliced thin
½ cup green pepper, diced
½ cup butter
⅓ cup flour
3 ½ cups milk
4 cups (1 pound) cheddar cheese, shredded

1 small jar diced pimento, drained

Simmer vegetables with bouillon cube or chicken-flavor vegetable mix until vegetables are tender. Melt butter in saucepan, blend in flour, cook one minute. Gradually add milk; cook over medium heat, stirring constantly. Add cheese, stirring until melted to create sauce. Stir cheese sauce and pimento into vegetable mixture. Cook over low heat until thoroughly heated (do not boil).

Gazpacho

Cautious as I was about trying new foods, I can remember how reluctant I was to taste a cold, uncooked soup for the first time. But after one bite, this recipe became one of my favorite summertime dishes.

6 medium-size tomatoes (about 2 pounds) peeled and chopped
1 medium size cucumber, pared and cut in chunks
1 large green pepper, seeded, and chopped
¼ cup lemon juice
1 cup water
¼ cup olive oil
½ teaspoon salt
¼ teaspoon freshly ground black pepper
½ cup green pepper, chopped
optional: cucumber, sliced

Combine ingredients in blender and blend until smooth. Garnish soup with cucumber and green peppers.

For a thinner, clearer soup, press ingredients through sieve.

For a thicker soup, add 2 slices of white bread, crumbled, and 2 cups tomato juice.

Cauliflower-Potato Soup

You think you don't like cauliflower? Prepare to be delighted.

3 cups potatoes, cubed
3 cups cauliflower, cut into florets
1 tablespoon butter or margarine
½ teaspoon nutmeg
1 teaspoon salt
⅛ teaspoon pepper
liquid from cooked vegetables
optional: ½ pound soft tofu, cut into chunks

Boil potatoes and cauliflower. Place vegetables, tofu, spices, and sufficient liquid in a blender and blend until smooth. (You will probably have to do this in two operations to get this quantity of vegetables blended.) Add liquid from cooking to make soup desired consistency. Serve hot.

For extra nutrition, blend soft tofu into the soup and reheat.

Corn Chowder

½ pkg. frozen or 1 cup fresh corn
½ cup chopped celery
4 medium potatoes, cooked; dice half, purée half
4 tablespoons flour
4 cups milk
½ teaspoon paprika
¼ teaspoon black pepper
½ teaspoon nutmeg
¼ teaspoon thyme
¼ teaspoon oregano
butter and salt to taste

Steam potatoes and corn. Set aside. Sauté celery in butter with spices. Stir in flour, add milk then cook 5 to 10 minutes, stirring frequently. Purée half the potatoes and half the corn, then add four/butter/celery/spice mixture. Add remaining potatoes and corn, mix well. For thinner chowder, add more milk or water.

Butternut Squash Soup

I'm amazed now at the number of things I was reluctant to try, including this delicious soup. The idea of making soup out of squash sounded weird, but at least my mind was open enough to try it. When I did try it, I loved it.

Any squash can be made into a soup but I like the delicate flavor of Butternut best. And, it's so easy.

One butternut squash
Sufficient milk or water for preferred thickness
Butter to taste
Nutmeg to taste

Steam or boil squash until tender. It's easy to remove skins if you've cooked the squash with them on. Cook, cool to handle, remove skins, then blend or mash the squash until smooth. Add milk, butter and spice. Blend until smooth. To make a thicker, smoother soup, make a flour roux and cook into the mixture.

Other soups:

See the Chapter on Beans (page 87) for:

- Pepper Pot Soup
- Pepper post soup with Barley
- Black Bean Soup

- Black Bean Soup with Barley
- Italian White Bean Soup

See chapter on **Vegetables** (page 141) for:

- Borscht
- Navy Bean 'Tater Soup
- Fruit soups

See the **Breakfast** chapter (page 163) for:

- Fruit soups

CHAPTER 18
Dressings, Sauces, Gravies

"You're right, homemade is better!"

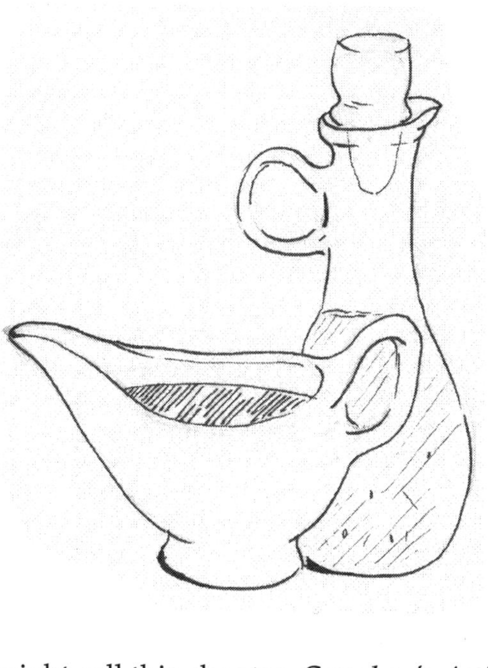

We might call this chapter, *Grandma's Attic* because it is full of all kinds of interesting odds and ends that we may at first not see their value. But when we give these a deeper look, we may suddenly realize we've found some treasures. For instance, one woman was ready to throw out a cheap purse belonging to her aunt's estate when she noticed a dull-colored chain in the bottom. It turned out to be a gold chain for a watch fob that was worth about $20,000.

Salad dressing is a good culinary example of how we may overlook something of value. Years ago I didn't much care for salads so I naturally passed over the recipes for dressings. But after I experimented with homemade dressings, I found they made salads fabulous. Let's face it, homemade is soooo much tastier. Store-bought dressings all seem to have the same underlying taste because most of them are made from cheap-as-possible common ingredients like vinegar and partial foods such as whey, various cheaper oils, and other not-best ingredients. With your own chemical-free, whole-food dressings you may find you suddenly have a whole new interest in "rabbit food."

Dressings

The secret ingredient in my recipes is lemon juice. It costs a little more than vinegar, but lemon tastes better and Ayurveda says it's better for health. Also, I only use olive oil—it's healthier and tastier than the more common vegetable oils.

Italian Herbal Salad Dressing

This may, as it did for me, turn out to be your favorite dressing.

1 cup vegetable or olive oil
¼ cup lemon juice
1 teaspoon ground fennel (for a sweeter taste with no calories, add up to 1 teaspoon extra fennel, and/or 1 tablespoon whole fennel)
½ teaspoon savory
½ teaspoon basil

¼ teaspoon thyme
½ teaspoon salt
2 tablespoons honey

Mix or blend well and allow to sit overnight, refrigerated.

Spring Herb Salad Dressing

1 cup cottage cheese
1 cup sour cream
½ cup water
½ cup oil
¼ cup lemon juice
1 tablespoon honey
¼ teaspoon salt
⅛ teaspoon pepper
1 teaspoon dried or one large bunch fresh dill
¼ teaspoon basil
¼ teaspoon tarragon
¼ teaspoon marjoram

Mix all ingredients in blender. Blend just until mixed well.

Creamy Sunflower Seed Dressing

1 teaspoon dried or 1 tablespoon fresh parsley
½ teaspoon dill
dash pepper
¼ teaspoon cumin
¼ teaspoon peppermint
¼ teaspoon salt
1 tablespoon honey
1 teaspoon lemon juice
½ cup sunflower seeds
⅓ cup water
1 cup oil

Blend ingredients until smooth.

Marinades

Use marinades for tofu, beans, vegetables, or bread cubes, the same way you'd use them for meat. Tofu doesn't absorb deep into itself so if you want more marinade taste, use smaller pieces.

Italian Marinade

1 teaspoon basil
1 teaspoon thyme
¼ teaspoon black pepper
¼ cup soy sauce
1 tablespoon lemon juice
¼ cup olive oil
½ cup water

Mix or blend ingredients.

"Lamb" Marinade

2 teaspoons lemon juice
¼ teaspoon cloves
salt to taste
¼ green pepper, diced small
2 teaspoon coriander
1 teaspoon cumin
1 teaspoon ginger
4 tablespoons oil
½ cup water

Mix or blend ingredients.

Sauces and Pastes

Guacamole

2 ripe avocados, mashed fine
¼ cup dairy sour cream (or ¼ cup tofu sour cream from recipe below)
1 tomato, peeled and chopped fine
1 tablespoon lemon juice
1 teaspoon salt
½ teaspoon chili powder

Combine all ingredients and mix well.

Tofu Substitute for Sour Cream

1/ 2 pound soft tofu
¼ cup oil
2 Tablespoons lemon juice
1 ½ teaspoon honey or sugar
½ teaspoon salt

Blend ingredients in blender until smooth.

Homemade Salsa

1 (16-ounce) can tomato sauce
½ cup green pepper, minced
1 tablespoons homemade chili/taco powder (page 227) or prepared taco spices to taste
½ teaspoon oregano
1 teaspoon cumin
¼ teaspoon pepper

Combine all ingredients and mix well.

Homemade Tomato Sauce

At least once, try making your own tomato sauce. You may never want to buy it again.

1 green pepper
1 carrot, sliced
1 stalk celery
12 teaspoons basil
1 teaspoon thyme
¼ cup minced parsley
¼ cup olive oil
9 cups chopped tomatoes
¼ cup water
2 bay leaves
1 teaspoon salt
1 to 2 teaspoons sugar

Sauté pepper, carrot, and celery. Add remaining ingredients. Cook until vegetables are tender and the taste is smooth. Oregano and/or zucchini may be added for variety or preference.

Basic Cream Sauce (Béchamel Sauce)

2 tablespoon butter
2 tablespoon flour
½ teaspoon salt
⅛ teaspoon nutmeg
1 cup milk

Using a whisk, stir the flour into heated butter and cook until mixture bubbles. Add salt and nutmeg; slowly add milk. Cook until smooth and thickened, stirring occasionally.

Spaghetti/Pizza Sauce

It's hard to find time to spend cooking but I found out why the Italians cooked their pastas for hours—it's at least in part because long cooking takes the sharp acidic taste out of the tomatoes, leaving a smoother, sweeter, richer flavor. This recipe calls for canned, but if you use your own homemade tomato sauce in this recipe, the results will be even more delicious.

1 (16-ounce) can tomatoes, diced
1 6-ounce can tomato paste
2 tablespoons olive oil
2 tablespoons oregano
2 ½ tablespoons basil
1 teaspoon sugar
salt and pepper to taste
½ teaspoon peppermint
1 cup water

Mix ingredients and simmer, stirring frequently to avoid sticking. If you don't have the time for long cooking, just heat and serve. By the way, the pinch of peppermint helps to prevent the flatulence that some folks get from eating pizza or spagetti.

Sweet and Sour Sauce

Sweet and sour sauces are perfect complements to Oriental foods, or add a bit of pizzazz to any meal.

1 can apricot or peach preserves, or cranberry sauce
1 teaspoon lemon juice
1 tablespoon arrowroot
½ cup water, add slowly
½ teaspoon salt
½ teaspoon cinnamon
¼ teaspoon ginger root
¼ teaspoon cloves
2 teaspoons vegetable oil

Simmer 5 to 10 minutes, add arrowroot and continue to cook until thick, stirring constantly.

Gravies

Celery Gravy

I still remember how excited I was when I discovered this gravy. Until I found it, I thought that to get a good gravy one had to use a meat base.

butter or oil
½ cup celery
1 teaspoon celery seed
2 tablespoons flour
2 cups water, boiling
¼ teaspoon sage
¼ teaspoon marjoram
¼ teaspoon thyme
salt and pepper to taste

Sauté celery in butter along with seeds and herbs, salt and pepper. Mix flour into the mixture and stir until slightly browned, then beat in water. Continue cooking, stirring frequently, until thickened.

"Beef" Gravy

Even your most macho guest may not realize this gravy isn't made from beef.

4 tablespoons oil
½ teaspoon black pepper
1 teaspoon cumin
1 teaspoon coriander
3 tablespoons flour
¼ cup soy sauce
3 cups water

Add flour and spices to oil heated over medium heat. Stir until slightly browned. Add soy sauce and water and continue cooking until thickened.

"Chicken" (Cauliflower Cream) Gravy

1 ½ cups potatoes, cubed
1 ½ cups cauliflower, cut into florets
1 tablespoon butter or margarine
½ teaspoon nutmeg
1 teaspoon salt
¼ teaspoon pepper
liquid from cooked vegetables

Optional: ¼ to ½ pound soft tofu, cut into chunks

Boil potatoes and cauliflower. In blender, blend vegetables, (tofu if desired), and spices, with enough liquid to blend until smooth. Add sufficient liquid from cooking to make gravy to desired consistency.

Etceteras

Most of us don't realize that the things we are in habit of buying pre-prepared can be made tastier and often less expensively at home.

Tahini Sauce

1 cup sesame seeds
2 tablespoons oil
½ cup water
1 teaspoon salt
¼ cup lemon juice

Blend ingredients in blender until seeds are fine. Add more water if necessary.

Ghee

Ancient wisdom says that ghee (clarified butter) is a fine medicine, good for all bodily functions taken internally or rubbed on any part of the body. Even without refrigeration, ghee will keep for months (some people say years) and it has a higher smoking point than vegetable oils.

To make ghee, simmer 1 pound unsalted butter for 20- 40 minutes or until the milk solids have separated and formed curds. Strain through cheesecloth and discard residue. If some residue gets into the butterfat, freezing will cause it to separate. Throw away the curds (or use it as suet for birds).

Pineapple Chutney

Add a dollop of chutney on any plate to give the meal a kick of taste. Like tomatoes, the long cooking of pineapple removes the sharp taste and emphasizes natural sweetness. Or, if you are short on time, it's still tasty if all you do is just mix, heat and stir.

1 (16-ounce) can crushed pineapple
½ teaspoon cumin
½ teaspoon ginger
¼ teaspoon ground cloves or sprinkle with 1 teaspoon whole cloves
¼ teaspoon curry
⅓ cup raisins
1 teaspoon ghee
water as needed to keep pineapple moist

Sauté spices and add to mixture. Mix well with other ingredients and cook until the raisins are plump.

Coriander Chutney

There are many ways to prepare chutney, with each way being better than the last. Start with this simple recipe then look on the Internet or in East Indian cookbooks for more.

1 cup fresh coriander leaves (cilantro)
1-2 fresh or pickled green chilies, or to taste
¼ teaspoon cumin
1 tablespoon lemon juice
pinch of sugar

Bend ingredients into a smooth paste.

Curried Apple Chutney

½ quart apples, peeled, cored, and chopped (about 4 medium)
½ pound seedless raisins
½ cup brown sugar
¼ cup sweet red pepper, chopped
¼ tablespoon mustard seed
½ tablespoon ginger
½ teaspoons allspice
½ teaspoon curry powder
½ teaspoon salt, or to taste
½ hot red pepper, chopped (wear gloves to seed and cut)
1-2 cloves of garlic, minced
1 cup lemon juice

Combine and simmer all ingredients until thick, stirring frequently to prevent sticking.

Refrigerate leftover chutney to spice up other meals.

Vata Tea

Bet you didn't know you can make your own teas. From Ayruveda, this tea it is not only delicious, it's soothing. I like to let it steep for 15-30 minutes to get the full flavor.

5 parts licorice root
2 ½ parts ginger
2 parts cardamom
1 part cinnamon

Store extra in a jar until you want tea, then put a little in a tea ball in boiling water.

CHAPTER 19
Herbs & Spices

"Our first line of defense against culinary boredom."

When I first began cooking with herbs, I felt overwhelmed with mystery. Which herbs go with what dish? Are spices added before or after cooking? How much should I use?

You may have questions like this too, but not to worry. Herbs and spices have been used since 10,000 BCE, and even though there was a time when panic over these questions would have been appropriate (until recent times, their cost was often equivalent to gold), today we can buy them in any super-market for a few dollars. And learning to use them is easy.

Now that you are a culinary adventurer, you will probably find, as I did, that you'll catch on quickly and after a little experimentation you'll suddenly find yourself able to taste-test the pot and say, "Ah, yes, this is good but I think it needs a pinch of .... "

Tips for Cooking with Herbs

- Dried herbs are stronger than fresh; powdered herbs are stronger than crumbled. A useful formula is: 1 teaspoon ground herbs equals 1 tablespoon minced fresh herbs.
- A mortar and pestle and a little seed grinder can be handy to free the aroma from dry herbs, and to grind seeds and make mixtures.
- Too much herbs can much can make a dish taste bitter or "muddy." Experiment until you get a feel for balance.
- Add herbs to soups or stews generally *no more than* 45 minutes before completing the cooking. (Extended cooking can cause herbs to lose their flavor or become bitter.) In contrast, for cold foods such as dips, cheese, vegetables, and dressing, herbs should be added several hours or overnight before using.

> **Helpful Hint:** ***to take accumulated grease and dust off your herb and spice jars, use baking soda and water.***

The following lists of herbs and spices are tools for beginners and a resource for developing new ideas of your own.

These are not the only options but it's a good base from which to begin. You may find that with experience, you can think of some pretty creative ways of mixing tastes together.

Herb & Spice Chart

Over time, it has been found that some tastes are "friendly" to each other; that is, complementary or enriching. The following chart is a list of herbs/spices that have made lasting friendships with certain foods.

Food	**Herbs and Spices**
Asparagus	cayenne, sesame seed
Beans, white	savory
Beets	ginger
Bread	caraway, thyme, marjoram, oregano, poppy seed, rosemary
Broccoli	cayenne, cinnamon, oregano, thyme
Brussels Sprouts,	sage, thyme
Cabbage	caraway, dill, oregano
Carrots	bay leaves, ginger, nutmeg, mace, parsley
Cauliflower	basil, celery seed, caraway, dill, nutmeg, mace, paprika
Chowder	basil, seafood mixes
Cheese	basil, chervil, dill, chives, curry, fennel, marjoram, oregano, parsley, sage, thyme
Corn.	sage
Cottage Cheese	allspice, mint, poppy seed
Dahls	curry, cumin, poppy seed, turmeric, coriander
Eggplant	allspice, cayenne, sage, coriander, basil
Fruit	anise, cinnamon, coriander, cloves, rose geranium, lemon verbena, mint, ginger
Green Salads	basil, marjoram

Kidney beans	chili powder
Lentils	celery seed, oregano, paprika, chili powder and other Mexican spices and herb blends
Lima Beans	sage
Okra	celery seed
Peas, green	mint, mustard
Potatoes	bay leaves, curry, marjoram, paprika, caraway
Rice	cloves, parsley, cardamom, turmeric
Soups	bay leaves, chervil, tarragon, savory, marjoram, parsley, rosemary
Spinach	marjoram, nutmeg, mace
Squash, Pumpkin	basil, nutmeg, cloves, marjoram, oregano, mace, cardamom, cinnamon
Sweet Potatoes	cinnamon, cloves, allspice
Tomatoes	basil, bay leaves, marjoram, oregano
Turnip	poppy seed, sesame seed
Vegetables, cooked	basil, chervil, chives, dill, mint, tarragon, curry, marjoram, pepper, parsley, thyme, rosemary

Herbs and Spices for Salad Dressings

Dressing	Herbs and Spices
Aspic	basil, bay leaves, marjoram, rosemary
Coleslaw	caraway seed, celery seed
French	allspice, bay leaves, cayenne, mustard, paprika, sage
Fruit	cardamom, celery seed, cinnamon, cloves, ginger, nutmeg, mace
Herb	marjoram, sage, rosemary, thyme
Italian	oregano, basil, thyme, savory, parsley
Dressing for Potato Salad	caraway seed, celery seed
Russian	basil
Sour Cream	chili powder, curry, dill
Tossed green	basil, marjoram

Herbs and Spices for Meat Flavors and Meat Type Dressings

Often it is not the meat itself we miss, but the flavorings. Try adding these flavors to tofu or other recipes to get the tastes you like.

To get this Flavor:	Use these Spices and Herbs:
Barbeque Sauce	cardamom, cayenne, cinnamon, rosemary
Beef and Beef Stews	allspice, bay leaves, caraway, cloves, cumin, pepper, marjoram, rosemary, savory
Chicken, poultry	sage, marjoram, rosemary, basil, curry, oregano, savory, prepared poultry seasonings
Gravies	celery seed, chili powder, thyme, sage, prepared gravy mixtures (read labels carefully)
Fish	chervil, dill, fennel, tarragon, parsley, thyme, lemon and lemon pepper, prepared mixtures
Lamb	basil, marjoram, oregano, rosemary, thyme
Pork	coriander, cumin, ginger, pepper, sage, savory, thyme
Sausage	sage, celery seed, nutmeg, mace
Shrimp Creole	basil, cayenne, prepared mixes
Stuffing	caraway seeds, celery seeds, marjoram, prepared poultry spices
Veal	basil

Favorite International Flavorings

German, European	caraway
Mexican	coriander, cilantro (fresh coriander leaves), cumin, oregano
India	coriander, cilantro, cumin, cardamom, fenugreek, ginger, cloves
Italian	basil, marjoram, oregano
Middle East	cumin, coriander

On Onions and Garlic, Fungus And Fermentation

None of the recipes in **The Reluctant Vegetarian** *call for mushrooms, vinegar, onion or garlic. If you don't want to give up these foods then simply add them to any recipe.*

Alternatives:

- *To replace vinegar: use lemon juice. My experience has been that lemon juice is not only tastier, but that it also requires less sweetener to achieve a balanced taste. (According to the University of Iowa Extension Center and my own experience, you can even replace vinegar in home canning with lemon juice.)*
- *To replace onions: Bok Choy makes an excellent substitute. Cut or cook it as you would onion in dishes, sandwiches or salads. Green peppers are another useful substitute.*
- *To replace garlic: Use a pinch of hing (asafetida). Use sparingly.*
- *As for mushrooms, an herbed white sauce can sometimes replace mushroom soup but, in all honesty, I simply haven't found a practical substitute for mushrooms.*

Odds and Ends of Useful Information about Herbs

- **Caraway,** bitter if cooked for more than one hour.
- **Cardamom,** natural breath freshener, good for the heart.
- Sauté **cumin** to bring out full flavor and keep it from tasting bitter or muddy in the dish.
- **Fenugreek** is often a major ingredient in curry powder, also good in salad dressings.
- **Turmeric** is a major ingredient in curry, but like cumin, it is best when sautéed first.

- **Italian Blend**: Mix Basil, marjoram, oregano, rosemary, sage, savory, thyme
- **Barbecue blend**: Cumin, garlic or hing, hot pepper, oregano
- **Bouquet garnish mixtures**: Bay , parsley, thyme. The herbs may be wrapped around the thyme and bay leaf.

Herb Recipes to Replace Salt

Spicy Seasoning

1 teaspoon each cloves, pepper and coriander seed (crushed)
2 teaspoons paprika
1 tablespoon rosemary

Mix ingredients in blender. Store in airtight container.

Spice Salt

1 ½ teaspoons each powdered thyme, bay leaf, black pepper, and nutmeg
¾ teaspoon cayenne
¾ teaspoon marjoram
3 teaspoons powdered cloves
3 teaspoons salt

Crush ingredients with a mortar and pestle. Sift together and mix thoroughly with amount of salt desired. If desired, put herbs in blender and process at low speed. Blend in the salt.

Variations: Celery salt is a good basic either alone or with other spices. Paprika, red pepper and dry mustard add color as well as flavor.

Other seasoning options: You will find a wide variety of seasoning salts and herb mixtures available in the herb and spice section of your grocery store.

Note: if you find the prices of seasonings too expensive at the supermarket, or if they get old before you use them up, you can get them less expensively and in smaller quantities at health food or farm stores that carry them in bulk.

Other Home Prepared Spice Mixtures

Basic Curry Powder

3 teaspoons turmeric
1 teaspoon cardamom
1 teaspoon coriander
1 teaspoon cumin
½ teaspoon cayenne pepper
½ teaspoon ginger

Mix well. Note: proportions can be altered to suit your tastes.

Graham Masala

Graham Masala is essentially a curry but is sweeter tasting.

1 teaspoon cumin
1 teaspoon ground cloves,
1 teaspoon ground bay leaves
1 teaspoon cardamom
1 teaspoon cinnamon
1 teaspoon pepper
½ teaspoon mace
½ teaspoon ginger

Mix well and use in any dish calling for curry powder.

Chili/Taco Powder

4 teaspoons cumin
3 teaspoons coriander
3 teaspoons paprika
1 teaspoon turmeric
1 teaspoon cloves
1 teaspoon oregano
1 teaspoon black pepper

Mix well.

MENU

CHAPTER 20
Menus

"Ah, Happy Tummy."

Creating vegetarian menus is not vastly different from creating meat menus, except that the protein main dish comes from a vegetable or other non-meat source. Begin by selecting any vegetarian main dish—meaning one with beans, peas, soy, cheese and dairy, grains, nuts or seeds—then add soups, salads, side dishes, and desserts just as you would for a meat meal.

Remember the **Rule of Tongue for Nutrition**: Eat a variety of foods. Don't eat the same thing every day. Assemble a pretty plate using different colored foods. Eat some foods that are cooked and some that are raw, with a pleasant balance of different textures. Above all, eat fresh foods, preferably organic but at least local.

Here are a few sample menus to get you started.

Sample Menus

Add salads or fresh vegetables such as carrot sticks, lettuce leaves, radish or tomato slices, and some fresh fruit to the following menu suggestions.

Dahl and Rice - page 98
Pour dahl over rice or serve on the side; sprinkle with diced fresh avocados

Benarasi Cauliflower . . . . .page 146
Pineapple Chutney . . . . .page 217
Chapattis (Flat breads or tortilla shells), warmed
Vata Tea . . . . .page 218

Four Seasons Casserole - page 141

Steamed vegetable
Three Bean Salad . . . . page 93

Tofu "Hamburger" Stuffed Peppers - page 73

Corn
Celery Soup . . . . .page 199

Fried Tofu Slices with Barbeque Sauce - page 196
served as is or in sandwiches

Sharalyn's Tomato Veggie Soup . .page 198
or
Italian Bean Soup. . . . . .page 99
Cornbread. . . . . .page 139
Cole Slaw or Salad

Stuffed Cheese/Rice Tomatoes - page 152

Green Beans
Cucumber Slices with Lemon and Pepper
Ranch Apple Cake. . . . . .page 135

Stir Fries with Tofu - page 61

Rice

Sweet and Sour Sauce ....page 214
(or sweetened cranberries)

Cookies

Okra Dokey with Tofu - page 154

Sweet Potato Pie ....page 155

Carrot and radish sticks

Rolled Cabbage Leaves Stuffed with Rice - page 105

Buttered Carrots

Sliced tomatoes with Home-made
Italian Dressing...........page 208

Tofu Meat Balls - page 68

Rice with Carrots.............page 125

Tabouli ....page 151

Hearty Meals for Meat and Potato Tastes

Tofu Beefsteak smothered with "beef" gravy - page 79

mashed potatoes

peas or green beans

Tofu Italian Meat Loaf - page 75

Mashed Potatoes

Celery or "Beef" gravy

peas

Tofu "Hamburger" Sloppy Joes - page 74

Baked potatoes or French fries

Corn on the Cob

Lentil Tacos with Fixings - page 91

Gazpacho .... .page 203

Pudding .... .page 175

By now you know you can use your own favorite menus simply by adding a vegetarian protein dish in place of the meat.

Sister site for more recipes: www.reluctantveggies.com

For more about nutrition: www.nutritionbynatalie.com

For more about Ayurveda: www.alltm.org/ayurveda.html

My web site: www.freshfoodsings.com.

Afterword

"Thanks for Doing the Right Thing"

"Art is limited," says a Japanese chef in a *National Geographic* article on tofu, "but the taste of nature is unlimited." Thank you for reading my book and sharing my experiences. I hope you feel not only less reluctant now but have become a "seasoned"' culinary traveler who has become aware that we are not limited to old favorites. You know now that opening ourselves to the "taste of nature," by being willing to experiment, we open our horizons and expand the range of our enjoyment.

Happy Eating!

Bibliography

Here are a few of the many vegetarian cookbooks worth reading.

MIRIAM KASIN HOSPADAR. **Heaven's Banquet: Vegetarian Cooking for Lifelong Health the Ayurveda Way.** Plume, 2001.

MIRIAM KASIN. **The Age of Enlightenment Cookbook**. Arco Publishers, 1980

LAPPE, FRANCES MOORE. **Diet for a Small Planet**. Ballentine Books, 1991.

SHANDLER, NINA AND MICHAEL. **How to Make All the Meat that You Eat Out of Wheat**. Atheneum, 1980

DANDER, HELEN. **The Best of the Zucchini Recipes Cookbooks**. Sterling Cookbooks, 1988 (P.O. Box 16, Pendel, PA 19047)

ROBERSTON, LAUREL. **Laurel's Kitchen The New Laurel's Kitchen: A Handbook for Vegetarian Cookery and Nutrition.** Ten Speed Press, 1986

COTTRELL, EDYTH YOUNG. **The Oats, Peas, Beans & Barley Cookbook**. TEACH Services, January 2004

Sister site for more recipes: www.reluctantveggies.com

For more about nutrition: www.nutritionbynatalie.com

For more about Ayurveda: www.alltm.org/ayurveda.html

My web site: www.freshfoodsings.com.

Author Biography

The author lives in Fairfield, Iowa, on a two acre farm where she raises veggies, pet chickens and Nigerian Dwarf milk goats.